The Political Economy of Noncompliance

The Political Economy of Noncompliance explains why states fail to comply with international law.

Over the last sixty years, states have signed treaties, established international courts and other supranational institutions to achieve the benefits of international cooperation. Nowhere has this been more successful than in the European Union. European integration has produced one of the most intensely legalized regimes in the world. Yet, even in the European Union, states often fail to comply with the law. This book explores the sources of and reasons for noncompliance, and assesses why noncompliance varies across the Member States by looking at the domestic politics of complying with international law. The author uses examples from the history of economic integration in the EU in three countries and two different policy areas to demonstrate these mechanisms at work.

The Political Economy of Noncompliance will be of interest to students and scholars of European politics, international relations and political economy.

Scott Nicholas Siegel is Assistant Professor of Political Science in the Department of National Security Affairs at the Naval Postgraduate School in Monterey, CA.

Routledge Advances in European Politics

1 **Russian Messianism**
Third Rome, revolution, Communism and after
Peter J.S. Duncan

2 **European Integration and the Postmodern Condition**
Governance, democracy, identity
Peter van Ham

3 **Nationalism in Italian Politics**
The stories of the Northern League, 1980–2000
Damian Tambini

4 **International Intervention in the Balkans since 1995**
Edited by Peter Siani-Davies

5 **Widening the European Union**
The politics of institutional change and reform
Edited by Bernard Steunenberg

6 **Institutional Challenges in the European Union**
Edited by Madeleine Hosli, Adrian van Deemen and Mika Widgrén

7 **Europe Unbound**
Enlarging and reshaping the boundaries of the European Union
Edited by Jan Zielonka

8 **Ethnic Cleansing in the Balkans**
Nationalism and the destruction of tradition
Cathie Carmichael

9 **Democracy and Enlargement in Post-Communist Europe**
The democratisation of the general public in fifteen Central and Eastern European countries, 1991–1998
Christian W. Haerpfer

10 **Private Sector Involvement in the Euro**
The power of ideas
Stefan Collignon and Daniela Schwarzer

11 **Europe**
A Nietzschean perspective
Stefan Elbe

12 **European Union and E-Voting**
Addressing the European parliament's internet voting challenge
Edited by Alexander H. Trechsel and Fernando Mendez

13 **European Union Council Presidencies**
A comparative perspective
Edited by Ole Elgström

14 **European Governance and Supranational Institutions**
Making states comply
Jonas Tallberg

15 **European Union, NATO and Russia**
Martin Smith and Graham Timmins

16 **Business, The State and Economic Policy**
The case of Italy
G. Grant Amyot

17 **Europeanization and Transnational States**
Comparing Nordic central governments
Bengt Jacobsson, Per Lægreid and Ove K. Pedersen

18 **European Union Enlargement**
A comparative history
Edited by Wolfram Kaiser and Jürgen Elvert

19 **Gibraltar**
British or Spanish?
Peter Gold

20 **Gendering Spanish Democracy**
Monica Threlfall, Christine Cousins and Celia Valiente

21 **European Union Negotiations**
Processes, networks and negotiations
Edited by Ole Elgström and Christer Jönsson

22 **Evaluating Euro-Mediterranean Relations**
Stephen C. Calleya

23 **The Changing Face of European Identity**
A seven-nation study of (supra)national attachments
Edited by Richard Robyn

24 **Governing Europe**
Discourse, governmentality and European integration
William Walters and Jens Henrik Haahr

25 **Territory and Terror**
Conflicting nationalisms in the Basque country
Jan Mansvelt Beck

26 **Multilateralism, German Foreign Policy and Central Europe**
Claus Hofhansel

27 **Popular Protest in East Germany**
Gareth Dale

28 **Germany's Foreign Policy Towards Poland and the Czech Republic**
Ostpolitik revisited
Karl Cordell and Stefan Wolff

29 **Kosovo**
The politics of identity and space
Denisa Kostovicova

30 **The Politics of European Union Enlargement**
Theoretical approaches
Edited by Frank Schimmelfennig and Ulrich Sedelmeier

31 **Europeanizing Social Democracy?**
The rise of the party of European socialists
Simon Lightfoot

32 **Conflict and Change in EU Budgetary Politics**
Johannes Lindner

33 **Gibraltar, Identity and Empire**
E.G. Archer

34 **Governance Stories**
Mark Bevir and R.A.W Rhodes

35 **Britain and the Balkans**
1991 until the present
Carole Hodge

36 **The Eastern Enlargement of the European Union**
John O'Brennan

37 **Values and Principles in European Union Foreign Policy**
Edited by Sonia Lucarelli and Ian Manners

38 **European Union and the Making of a Wider Northern Europe**
Pami Aalto

39 **Democracy in the European Union**
Towards the emergence of a public sphere
Edited by Liana Giorgi, Ingmar Von Homeyer and Wayne Parsons

40 **European Union Peacebuilding and Policing**
Michael Merlingen with Rasa Ostrauskaite

41 **The Conservative Party and European Integration since 1945**
At the heart of Europe?
N.J. Crowson

42 **E-Government in Europe**
Re-booting the state
Edited by Paul G. Nixon and Vassiliki N. Koutrakou

43 **EU Foreign and Interior Policies**
Cross-pillar politics and the social construction of sovereignty
Stephan Stetter

44 **Policy Transfer in European Union Governance**
Regulating the utilities
Simon Bulmer, David Dolowitz, Peter Humphreys and Stephen Padgett

45 **The Europeanization of National Political Parties**
Power and organizational adaptation
Edited by Thomas Poguntke, Nicholas Aylott, Elisabeth Carter, Robert Ladrech and Kurt Richard Luther

46 **Citizenship in Nordic Welfare States**
Dynamics of choice, duties and participation in a changing Europe
Edited by Bjørn Hvinden and Håkan Johansson

47 **National Parliaments within the Enlarged European Union**
From victims of integration to competitive actors?
Edited by John O'Brennan and Tapio Raunio

48 **Britain, Ireland and Northern Ireland since 1980**
The totality of relationships
Eamonn O'Kane

49 **The EU and the European Security Strategy**
Forging a global Europe
Edited by Sven Biscop and Jan Joel Andersson

50 **European Security and Defence Policy**
An implementation perspective
Edited by Michael Merlingen and Rasa Ostrauskait

51 **Women and British Party Politics**
Descriptive, substantive and symbolic representation
Sarah Childs

52 **The Selection of Ministers in Europe**
Hiring and firing
Edited by Keith Dowding and Patrick Dumont

53 **Energy Security**
Europe's new foreign policy challenge
Richard Youngs

54 **Institutional Challenges in Post-Constitutional Europe**
Governing change
Edited by Catherine Moury and Luís de Sousa

55 **The Struggle for the European Constitution**
A past and future history
Michael O'Neill

56 **Transnational Labour Solidarity**
Mechanisms of commitment to cooperation within the European trade union movement
Katarzyna Gajewska

57 **The Illusion of Accountability in the European Union**
Edited by Sverker Gustavsson, Christer Karlsson, and Thomas Persson

58 **The European Union and Global Social Change**
A Critical geopolitical-economic analysis
József Böröcz

59 **Citizenship and Collective Identity in Europe**
Ireneusz Pawel Karolewski

60 **EU Enlargement and Socialization**
Turkey and Cyprus
Stefan Engert

61 **The Politics of EU Accession**
Turkish challenges and central European experiences
Edited by Lucie Tunkrová and Pavel Šaradín

62 **The Political History of European Integration**
The hypocrisy of democracy-through-market
Hagen Schulz-Forberg and Bo Stråth

63 **The Spatialities of Europeanization**
Power, governance and territory in Europe
Alun Jones and Julian Clark

64 **European Union Sanctions and Foreign Policy**
When and why do they work?
Clara Portela

65 **The EU's Role in World Politics**
A retreat from Liberal internationalism
Richard Youngs

66 **Social Democracy and European Integration**
The politics of preference formation
Edited by Dionyssis Dimitrakopoulos

67 **The EU Presence in International Organizations**
Edited by Spyros Blavoukos & Dimitris Bourantonis

68 **Sustainability in European Environmental Policy**
Challenge of governance and knowledge
Edited by Rob Atkinson, Georgios Terizakis and Karsten Zimmermann

69 **Fifty Years of EU-Turkey Relations**
A Sisyphean story
Edited by Armagan Emre Çakir

70 **Europeanization and Foreign Policy**
State Ddversity in Finland and Britain
Juha Jokela

71 **EU Foreign Policy and Post-Soviet Conflicts**
Stealth intervention
Nicu Popescu

72 **Switzerland in Europe**
Continuity and change in the Swiss political economy
Edited by Christine Trampusch and André Mach

73. **The Political Economy of Noncompliance**
Adjusting to the single European market
Scott Nicholas Siegel

The Political Economy of Noncompliance

Adjusting to the single European market

Scott Nicholas Siegel

Routledge
Taylor & Francis Group
LONDON AND NEW YORK

First published 2011
by Routledge
2 Park Square, Milton Park, Abingdon, Oxon, OX14 4RN

Simultaneously published in the USA and Canada
by Routledge
711 Third Avenue, New York, NY 10017

Routledge is an imprint of the Taylor & Francis Group, an informa business

British Library Cataloguing in Publication Data
A catalogue record for this book is available from the British Library

Library of Congress Cataloguing in Publication Data
A catalog record has been requested for this book

Siegel, Scott Nicholas, 1976–
The political economy of noncompliance : adjusting to the single European market / Scott Nicholas Siegel.
p. cm.
Includes bibliographical references and index.
1. International and municipal law–European Union countries.
2. European Union countries–Politics and government.
3. European federation–Economic aspects. 4. Government aid–European Union countries. I. Title.
KJE971.5.S56 2011
341.242'2–dc22 2011012046

ISBN: 978-0-415-61585-3 (hbk)
ISBN: 978-0-203-81632-5 (ebk)

Typeset in Times New Roman
By Glyph International

MIX
Paper from responsible sources
FSC® C004839

Printed and bound in Great Britain by the MPG Books Group

Contents

Figures and tables

Figures

Tables

Preface

This book examines the two-level game that governments must play when attempting to comply with international law. In a thoroughly globalized world, governments face serious tradeoffs. On the one hand, states participate in an international community. They cooperate with each other to solve major international problems, whether transnational terrorism, climate change or human trafficking. On the other hand, national leaders in modern democracies should be fulfilling the wishes and demands of a majority of voters. The tensions between complying with a country's international legal obligations and satisfying the will of a majority of its citizens are growing in number and in severity. Short of renegotiating international rules, governments have two choices before them. They can choose not to comply with their agreements and risk punishment by other members of the international community. Or they can choose to comply with an international rule and realize the benefits of cooperation, but then risk domestic backlash.

The debate over the role of international law and institutions in modern democracies has reached a particularly heightened stage in the European Union. Over sixty years of integration, EU rules and regulations play a significant role in the daily lives of its citizens. But even within a regime as legalized and integrated as the European Union, noncompliance occurs frequently. Whether the content of pasta or the size of budget deficits, EU law stands over the actions and policies of its Member States. Citizens and groups both within and outside the country stand ready to monitor compliance. Some groups push their governments to comply in order to make them better off. Others pull their governments away from complying to avoid significant harm. Most of the gains generating by compliance are significant, but spread across national society and over the long-term. In contrast, the costs of complying are usually concentrated among a small number of groups. These groups then mobilize to influence their governments and reach the European Court of Justice in Luxembourg. In most cases, if the ECJ's decision in the case is against the Member State, the Member State chooses to comply. The government has shown a proper amount of deference to domestic interests, but does not want to risk the losses that future cooperation would bring. But when no further cooperation appears on the horizon or the costs are high and shared by large groups in society, Member State governments will refuse to comply.

The interaction of different levels of politics produces four different types of compliance behavior. State behavior varies from complete compliance and swift change to the status quo to outright refusal. To show these different types of behavior, five cases of noncompliance with EU law are presented. Two cases relate to the free movement of goods in the EU in traditional national industries in Germany and France. Two other cases explore noncompliance in the sensitive areas of subsidies to domestic industries. While the German government attempted to maintain a key element of *Modell Deutschland*, the British government violated EU law in order to save its last domestic auto manufacturer. Even in these key areas of national interest, these governments chose to comply. But not all legal regimes in the EU are created equal. In the case of European Monetary Union, noncompliance was almost inevitable. Although eurozone members made significant strides in meeting the criteria for membership, violations of the rules governing membership occurred frequently. If noncompliance with EMU is placed within the framework of a collective action problem, we could see that the crisis that engulfed the eurozone in 2009 and 2010 was somewhat easy to predict.

This book's topic contributes to the growing debate over the legitimacy of international law in modern democracies. National governments must carefully navigate the ship of state between the threats of punishment and retaliation for not complying with their legal obligations and being held to account for ignoring the will of a democratic majority. Opposition does not just come from the electorate. Constitutional courts, political interest groups and ideological organizations also raise strong objections to the role of international law in domestic governance. In contrast, there are groups across both the developed and the developing world that see international law and compliance with it as a force for good in the world. When domestic governing institutions are insufficient or pursuing objectively harmful policies, international law can work to change the behavior of national leaders. Basically, just as national governments are facing a tradeoff between complying or not complying with international law, governments and citizens must decide between increasing output or input types of legitimacy. Do citizens want to inhibit the performance of international institutions by increasing their democratic accountability? Or do they wish to sacrifice democratic accountability in favor of more effective ways of solving international problems? This book makes a modest attempt at outlining the nature of that debate. Yet the results of that debate will ultimately be a function of politics, which should be a point of departure for additional research related to compliance with international law.

This book originated out of a dissertation written at Cornell University. There I received the strong support of Peter Katzenstein, Jonas Pontusson, Sidney Tarrow and Christopher Way. Residency and resources at the Wissenschaftszentrum Berlin enabled me to carry out important archival research and exchange my ideas with leading scholars in the field. In particular, I would like to thank Michael Zürn and everyone in the Department of Transnational

Conflicts and International Institutions for hosting me on multiple occasions. Both technological and travel support awarded to me by the Naval Postgraduate School's Research Initiation Program and other financial sources at NPS is also greatly appreciated. Lieve Cuypers generously satisfied my sometimes urgent requests for obscure data.

I would especially like to direct my gratitude towards my colleagues, friends and family who have been so patient and understanding throughout the past few years as this project moved from inception to completion. The friendships I forged at Cornell proved to be as enduring as expected, despite long gaps in time and space. Devashree Gupta, Stephen Watts and Andrew Phillips were always there to share mutual frustrations and joys. Jeff Knopf and Robert Weiner are wonderful colleagues and friends who kept my spirits up through pleasant lunch conversations and during the long commutes. My friends in Berlin, especially Martin Binder, made sure I lived a life that was properly balanced between work and play. My parents and siblings, Charles and Barbara and Mark and Crystal, supported me through difficult stretches, even if they did not always understand why the process seemed to be dragging on without end. Finally, I wish to dedicate this book to my partner in life and love, F. Landon Clark. The completion of this project would not have been possible without his strong words of encouragement and acts of deep caring. It is to him I dedicate this book.

1 Introduction

In January 2008, leaders of the 27 Member States of the European Union gathered in Berlin to mark the 50th anniversary of the Treaty of Rome. The celebration included exhibits, music concerts and speeches and closed with a fireworks display in front of the Brandenburg Gate. Although the celebration was in Berlin, because Germany was holding the EU presidency at the time, a more appropriate location could not have been chosen. Emerging from the ashes of destruction, Germany, together with France and four other countries, forged the Rome Treaty to secure a European peace that would be sustained for future generations. Integrating Germany into a European institutional framework ensured it could never threaten its neighbors again. And, therefore, many believed Europe would never be plunged back into war, avoiding the repeat of the deaths of millions. As such, the Treaty of Rome, or the EC Treaty, accomplished a key European diplomatic and geostrategic goal.

By setting the foundation stone for future cooperation, the Treaty of Rome is a remarkable historical achievement for all of Europe. The European Union today represents a degree of international economic and political cooperation unprecedented in world history. With some exceptions, most think that the EU represents a great victory for all of its citizens. But the anniversary celebration, justifiably, ignores all of the moments in which progress was stopped and those who opposed it. Among the first failures was the rejection of the European Defense Community by the French Parliament in 1954. Then General Charles de Gaulle's opposition to more supranational power for the EC led to the "empty chair" crisis in 1965. The United Kingdom's application to join was rejected twice. The Maastricht Treaty was rejected in a Danish referendum in 1992 and barely passed in France. Finally, despite widespread optimism among political elites, the Constitution failed in Holland and France in 2005. The Irish electorate rejected its successor, the Treaty of Lisbon, until a second referendum approved it in 2009.

Opposition to European integration has not just come at important historical moments. It also occurs through the frequent practice of attempting to enforce the EC Treaty and other types of EU law. The Commission, as the guardian of the Treaties, is charged with ensuring that the Member States and their citizens are adhering to EU law. The instances that it discovers when a Member State violates

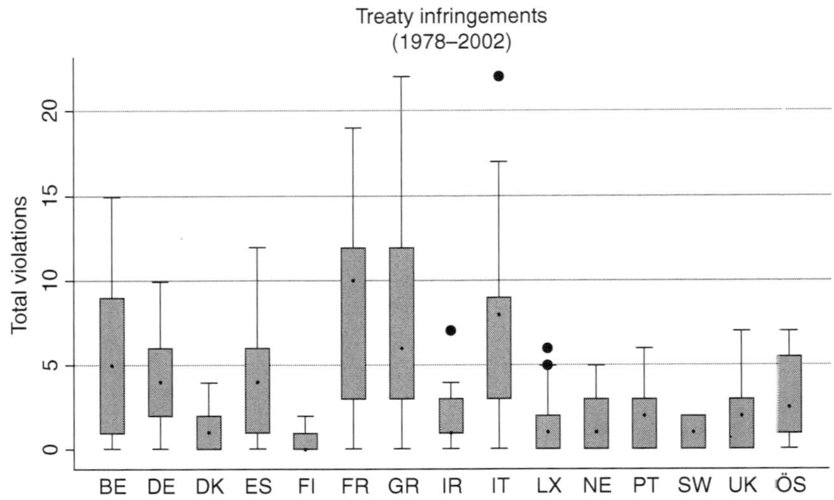

Figure 1.1 Cross-national distribution of EU legal violations.
Source: European Commission Annual Reports.

EU law serve as small illustrations of opposition or reluctance of a government to integrate fully. Despite the large collective gains European integration has produced, some countries choose to maintain the status quo more often and as long as they can more than others.

Figure 1.1 shows the cross-national variation in violations of EU law the Member States have committed just in the area of the EC Treaty and regulations based on it. Some of the most supportive members of the European project have violated the EC Treaty more than others that have been more skeptical. The single dot in the shaded box area represents the median number of infringements committed each year. The shaded areas surrounding the dot show the range of violations committed each year that fall within the range of the 25th and 75th percentile. The whiskers at each end encase the number of violations that occur each year that are within one quartile of this range. Marks outside the boxed areas represent the minimum and maximum number of violations committed in this time period.

For example, even though both Italy and Greece receive a substantial amount of funds from the EU to develop their poorer regions, they commit the largest number of violations. In contrast, despite a strong antipathy to supranational authority, the United Kingdom appears to comply more often than some of the EU's strongest supporters, such as Germany or France. In addition, some countries choose to delay complying with a suspected violation more than others. If the Commission discovers or confirms that a violation has taken place and the national government either does not reply or alter its behavior within the allotted time, the infringement case is referred to the European Court of Justice. Some countries are willing to risk an adverse ruling more than others (see Figure 1.2).

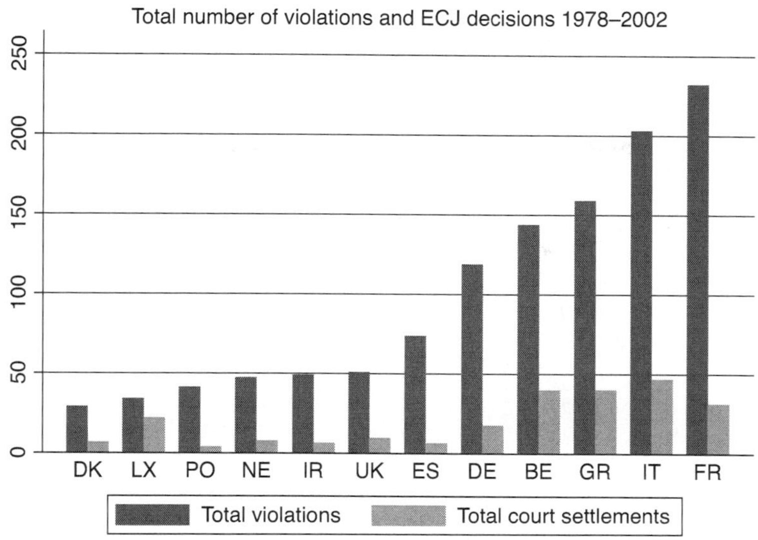

Figure 1.2 EU legal violations and ECJ decisions.
Source: European Commission Annual Reports.

The aim of this book is to provide a powerful but elegant model of noncompliance to account for why violations of EU law occur and why some violations escalate and are decided by the ECJ. Thus, noncompliance not only varies among the Member States of the EU, but with how governments choose to handle violations of EU law when they do occur.

More generally, these violations also show that political opposition to European integration has always existed and continues to grow. When national leaders wished, they withheld their support for more integration. When allowed, European voters expressed their disapproval at the ballot box. However, these moments are rare. Instead, most opposition to the policies of the European Union takes place through cases of noncompliance with EU law. By studying noncompliance and opposition to the process of European integration, this book sheds more light on the losers associated with European integration compared to the almost exclusive focus on the winners to this point.

The argument in brief

Despite the EU being one the most legalized regimes in the world, noncompliance occurs often. Although the European Commission and Court of Justice can punish states and individuals for noncompliance, violations still happen frequently. And there is a great amount of variation when they do. The number of violations committed varies across time and country. Some cases of noncompliance are settled sooner than others. Many suspected infringements are dismissed once Commission and national officials discuss them. On other occasions, albeit rare ones, a Member State is punished in the form of economic sanctions. This rich amount of diverse political behavior calls for an explanation that is comprehensive but yet parsimonious. This book aims to account for much of this variation by providing a simple but rigorous theory for why noncompliance occurs and why some legal violations are settled sooner than others.

What are the sources of noncompliance? Why does noncompliance vary across the Member States and over time? These questions are answered by looking at the domestic politics of international law. States face numerous countervailing political pressures when trying to comply with law beyond the nation state. On one side, international institutions, courts and even other regime members will call for a country to abide by its legal commitments. On the other side stand interest groups or other actors at the domestic level who demand their national governments not to comply in order to protect some economic or political advantage. Like many other issues in international politics, the situation resembles a two-level game.[1] How national governments react to these counteracting pressures is the subject of this book.

Drawing on basic theories of collective action, I argue that compliance with international law is a public good for a country. Hypothetically, every country that belongs to an international regime benefits when each member of the regime fulfills its international legal obligations. Governments comply with international law for several reasons. First, states did not construct these agreements unless they achieve some material or social gain for their members. By complying with them, they secure these gains. Second, if there is a likelihood of more cooperation in the future, governments will comply even though they may suffer some short-term losses in exchange for long-term gains. Third, a state can begin to enjoy the benefits to its general reputation such that other states will want to cooperate with it in the future if it is perceived as having a good reputation as a strong "team player."

Whether these benefits are actually realized depends on the type of public good and how it is produced. There are always dangers of free riding and thus the under- or even non-provision of the public good. Free riding is mostly likely to happen when the public good is nonrival and nonexclusive. It is considered nonrival if one member's consumption does not affect another's. It is nonexclusive when one or more members cannot be excluded from enjoying the public good without bearing high costs. Problems of coordination build up if the regime's members are of different sizes or have different levels of interest in the production of the public good. Unless a large member can produce enough of the public good that every member will enjoy, there is significant chance that too little of the public good will be provided, or none at all. Thus, members of international regimes create institutions to monitor agreements and to ensure that violators are punished. Only when the costs of cheating exceed its benefits will states choose to comply.

International organizations must secure a certain level of compliance in order for the public good to be produced. Thus, they are awarded the powers of sanctioning possible offenders (Axelrod and Keohane 1985, Downs *et al.* 1996, Olson 1965,

Underdal 1998). They also can provide incentives for states to comply through financial or technical assistance. Whether carrots or sticks are used to secure compliance summarizes the basic difference between the enforcement and management schools of compliance (Chayes *et al.* 1998, Young 1992). While monitoring and punishment are used to increase the costs of cheating, technical and financial assistance are used to help a country realize the benefit of cooperation.

There is a long debate over which method is most effective to secure compliance. Tallberg (2002) argues compliance is most likely to happen when the tools of both schools are used. But neither school examines why one method works in some circumstances and not in others. Whether a stick or a carrot works to secure compliance depends on the source of a government's calculus to comply. When a government will shirk its international legal responsibilities and when it will surrender to the wishes of its domestic constituents depends on how it weighs the costs and benefits based on factors at home. When a state achieves the goals of cooperation, those benefits usually benefit the entire country, but the costs of complying are concentrated among a small group of people. More importantly, the origins of noncompliance remain uninvestigated. For example, if we consider a ban on the use of chemical weapons on the battlefield or in general, national militaries as well as citizens will benefit if they are not used. However, the industries that produce and sell these weapons will suffer from a decline in demand for their products. These firms are then rationally motivated to ask their governments either to cheat or to shirk their international legal responsibilities.

Because the costs of compliance are usually concentrated, those groups opposed to compliance will pressure their governments to refrain from changing the status quo. They are usually the first ones to discover what the effects of compliance will be. They have strong incentives to monitor EU legislation to see how it will affect them. A Member State's regulations may not just be discriminating against the import of goods from another Member State. They are also protecting native industries or firms from European competition. As a result, those opposed to compliance become immediately aware of what state practices do not meet their country's legal obligations because they benefit the most from noncompliance.

Those groups who oppose compliance will form associations and lobby their governments to reject changes to the status quo demanded by international institutions or other regime members. They organize opposition by publicizing their disputes with their national governments. These groups stage rallies and generate sympathy from the surrounding public. They frame their arguments with national and European officials by characterizing their disputes as a struggle between national autonomy or sovereignty and the arbitrary actions of unelected, remote and, sometimes, illegitimate international institutions. While their true motivations lie in protecting their own self-interests, blaming international institutions for demanding undesired change often generates sympathy, such as when the IMF imposed austerity measures during the Asian financial crisis of the 1990s. They also can threaten to hold their nationally elected legislators to account by working for their defeat in future elections.

National governments then must make a difficult choice. They must navigate between the Charybdis of displeasing their domestic constituencies by complying with their international legal obligations and the Scylla of shirking their responsibility under international law. A government's choice between the two depends on the strength of domestic opposition and the carrots and sticks that international institutions threaten or offer to national governments to obtain their compliance. In some circumstances, when domestic opposition is strong, governments will not comply until an international court makes a ruling in the matter. Governments can then justify changes to the status quo that harm powerful constituents or interest groups as being necessary for several reasons. First, they may cite their general obligation to abide by international law, a norm that all modern states follow. Second, they are wary of sacrificing the long-term gains of future cooperation to satisfy the demands of a powerful domestic constituency. Third, governments could fear retaliatory actions by other regime members, whereby their countries' own goods and products are discriminated against. If governments choose to violate legal norms related to the treatment of prisoners of war, their own troops could face similar treatment by other countries or groups. Thus, not every government is willing to risk future increased costs or decreased benefits by refusing to comply.

There are circumstances in which governments can avoid this dilemma. First, governments can always comply immediately with their obligations. They comply either because their current policies satisfy their legal requirements or because domestic opposition to changing the status quo fails to materialize. Second, they can avoid the dilemma by refusing to comply at all. Governments can choose to maintain compliance either because the risk of offending domestic constituencies is too great, such as their own political survival, or the costs of compliance simply exceed the benefits as perceived at the time. For example, while states will commit to maintaining an exchange rate within a specific range of values, a change in international economic conditions or some other exogenous shock to the system, such as a severe financial crisis, can force governments to violate their previous agreements. None of the other incentives to maintain cooperation or disincentives to avoid defection will be effective.

The range of choices governments have in order to deal with conflicts between national policies and international law shows that state behavior is more than a simple dichotomy between compliance and noncompliance. Rather, state behavior ranges from complete compliance, or what I call obedience, to complete noncompliance, which I term refusal. In the case of the former, no changes to the national status quo are necessary for a state to satisfy its international legal obligations. In the case of the latter, a government will fail to comply despite any threats of punishment for defection or incentives to maintain its cooperation. In between, there are two other types of compliance behavior. The first, termed accommodation, is when important changes to the national status quo must be made to comply but domestic opposition fails to develop. As a result, compliance takes place swiftly and without difficulty. In contrast, the final and fourth type of compliance behavior is reluctance. Reluctance occurs when domestic opposition is strong and the government will refuse to comply until the stakes of noncompliance become too great. This may include disobeying an international court ruling, retaliatory behavior from other regime members, or the risk of jeopardizing future gains of cooperation. Chapter 2 unpacks more of the elements of each type of behavior. It also specifies the conditions under which each type of compliance behavior is expected and which institutional or political factors can lead to some types of behavior occurring in some countries more often than in others.

The sources of noncompliance

Why do violations of international law occur? The character of the violations depends on the type of actions an international agreement is either trying to foster or curtail. However, all violations happen because of some gap between the goals of an international agreement or law and current state behavior. The full consequences of an international agreement can rarely be anticipated. Regime signatories will attempt to specify the prescriptions and proscriptions associated with an agreement as effectively and precisely as they can. However, unanticipated consequences and unintended effects almost always occur because of the inherent limitations national leaders face in gauging the future effects of their actions. Incomplete information, vague legal language and general uncertainty lead to the discovery of new state practices that are not conforming to an international legal obligation.

In the case of the European Union, many violations occur as the regulatory barriers or special privileges firms enjoy from national regulations come under the scrutiny of the Commission. In an effort to complete the single internal market, the Commission grew increasingly skeptical of the efforts governments made to protect particular industries from European competition. Many of the quantitative barriers to EU trade had already fallen with the completion of the customs union. The Commission increasingly turned toward the qualitative regulatory barriers that discriminated against goods from other EU Member States. Yet those barriers secured a dominant position for particular firms or industrial sectors. For example, the requirement in Germany for all beer to be limited to four ingredients gave German brewers a decisive advantage within the German market.

Among the EU Member States, economic integration has already produced significant amounts of economic convergence among national industries such that relative prices are not the primary source of competition. Instead, competition is between groups of firms within the same industry along the lines of quality and taste or some non-quantitative advantage. For example, unfair trade advantages for domestic firms also occur because of special financial relationships with the state that serve as indirect subsidies. As competitive pressures grew, the regulatory practices that gave some groups of firms within a particular industry a specific trade advantage became subject to the Commission's scrutiny. In short, the multiple practices states use to protect their own firms from

European competition are the source of most legal infringements related to the single European market.

Through the development of EU case law, the European Commission created a robust legal doctrine that specified when these non-tariff barriers contradicted the EC Treaty. When there are few to no violations in a specific area, the state is in obedience. When the Commission determines a national regulation is distorting the smooth operation of the internal market, it launches an investigation. If the government chooses to change the status quo immediately, it is accommodating the Commission's legal demands. If the national government responds by justifying these laws under EU law, the case can lead to adjudication before the ECJ. While perhaps legally legitimate, these justifications often hide blatant economic or political interests the status quo. Groups defending these regulations can include firms, unions or social groups that will experience material or social loss as a result of their government complying with the Commission's request. If the government succumbs to domestic political pressure, it is reluctant to comply until the ECJ makes a definitive ruling, usually against the Member State. At this point, the threat of additional sanctions or the normative duty to obey European law will push a state to comply with the Commission's demands. In rare circumstances, however, this will not be sufficient to overcome domestic opposition and a government will choose to refuse to comply completely.

The state of the literature

The argument made in this book speaks to several areas of scholarship all at once. First, it engages the International Relations (IR) literature that relates to compliance with international law, from both rationalist and constructivist perspectives. Second, it draws on theories of international and comparative political economy to explain the political cleavages surrounding noncompliance in the European Union. Third, it extends current scholarship related to the politics of the EU regarding the implementation of EU law and the process of Europeanization.

Louis Henkin famously wrote, "It is probably the case that almost all nations observe almost all the principles of international law and almost all of their obligations almost all of the time" (Henkin 1979). Both social constructivist and rationalist approaches try to explain why this statement may or may not be true. Constructivist approaches focus on how norms, identities and even discursive practices generate compliance with international law. Each approach has its strengths and weaknesses. Not all of them can be addressed here. Instead, I focus on how my arguments about compliance fill in some important gaps in the literature.

Compliance and constructivism

International law, according to the social constructivist perspective, constitutes the international system and helps shape state behavior. First, some argue that international law is different from other norms in that it creates a sense of legal obligation (Reus-Smit 2003, 2004). The sense of a legal obligation defines what legitimate state behavior is and helps states decide what the normatively correct policy to follow is as well as the appropriate procedures or policies by which disputes between states should be solved. The English school sees international law as having a moral force of its own and helping to constitute international society (Bull 1977). As Thomas Franck (1995) argues, international law "pulls" states into compliance. Beside the general obligation to follow international legal norms, some rules are more likely to be complied with when they have higher degrees of specificity, durability and concordance, which affect the strength of a law's moral pull (Legro 1997).

Some states that hold a particular identity can shape the likelihood that they will comply with international law. For example, if a state's regime is democratic, then it is more likely to comply than an authoritarian state. Because democracies are accustomed to the rule of law and the due process of law to settle domestic disputes, they transfer these customs to the international arena and, therefore, are more likely to comply with an international rule than autocracies or semi-authoritarian regimes, whose actions are often solely egoistic or arbitrary (Slaughter 1995). Being democratic does not just imply that democracies will use prescribed procedures to decide whether to comply or not. Rather, a regime's type generates a particular culture of accepting the power of law's rationality rather than pure power or self-interest considerations to shape the government's actions.

Even when a state's cultural identity or the general norm of legal obligation is not at work, the actions of normative entrepreneurs can place political pressure on governments to comply. Epistemic communities of scientists and political activists operate through various networks to change the preferences or construct the interests of states such that they decide to comply with international rules (Haas 1992). These normative entrepreneurs can operate transnationally, such as international NGOs (Finnemore and Sikkink 1998, Keck and Sikkink 1998, Sikkink 1993) or organizations that operate primarily at the domestic level (Knopf 1998). These actors alert governments to problems of noncompliance, mobilize large groups and engage in social action to force their governments to comply while also advancing their own causes.

Finally, within the social constructivist paradigm, the practice of international law itself can produce compliance. Both legal scholars and political scientists highlight how the discursive nature of practicing international law explains why states comply. Rather than the norms themselves, the actual deliberative practice of discussing what international norms are will lead to rule-adhering behavior. Legal discourse places all parties to a dispute on an equal footing and forces governments to justify their claims and behavior through a set of reasons that flow logically from accepted legal principles, setting aside the instruments of power and interests (Kratochwil 1989). Harold Koh shows how the transnational legal process, beginning with discursive interaction, proceeding to interpretation and, finally, to internalization, generates compliance (Koh 1996, 1997). Studies that show the role of communicative action also demonstrate why states comply with international law (Panke 2007).

Yet, while these various theories within the social constructivist oeuvre explain why states comply, they cannot explain why Member States of the European Union are failing to comply. First, each Member State has been thoroughly socialized into the world in which international law has a moral and legitimate pull of its own. Second, all of the Member States can be considered robust democracies that respect the rule of law. There are also epistemic communities at work in the EU to secure compliance with EU law when it benefits them. Furthermore, neither of these theories can explain so far why compliance will vary within the same legal regime.

In summary, while social constructivist approaches so far tell us much about why states comply, they have not yet confronted issues related to noncompliance. Although this book uses a "soft" rational choice perspective to explain noncompliance, the theoretical framework here is compatible with a social constructivist approach. First, by focusing on the domestic politics of compliance, we can identify the actors that are most likely to oppose complying with an international norm. But, instead of acting for self-interested reasons, these "bad" social actors work to prevent states from complying because they do not share the same norms or do not believe international law is legitimate. These actors include war criminals, leaders of revolutionary movements, and even US Supreme Court justices. In some cases, they are able to influence their governments not to comply with international law, and not in others.

Rationalist approaches to compliance

Rationalist approaches to compliance, specifically the neoliberal institutionalist school, reframe the problem of compliance as one based on the logic of consequences rather than one of appropriateness (March and Olsen 1998). Instead of obeying international law because it is perceived as legitimate or acceptable state practice, states assess the relative utility of complying with the agreements they have constructed. The scholarly contributions in this area have been quite significant. This approach generates clear hypotheses as to why some states comply and others do not that are the basis for my argument. The major shortcoming of this literature is that it often confuses the behavioral outcome as the proximate cause. As with most functionalist explanations, the results observed are justified *post hoc* as the cause of the outcome.

The international factors that enhance cooperation with international law include a state's reputation, the likelihood of future gains, and tools of enforcement and detection that can shape a state's interests. First, if cooperation is modeled as a game of Prisoner's Dilemma, a state will comply when other parties do also. While they both have an incentive to defect, mutual defection brings on greater losses than if they had chosen to cooperate together. One solution is to have each actor play repeatedly over time (Axelrod 1984). If so, then a state can gain a reputation for being a cooperative player when it repeatedly complies with its international agreements.[2]

Yet, the tools of retaliation and an established reputation fail to work effectively when noncompliance cannot be detected or when disagreement exists among the parties as to whether suspect behavior conforms to the intent of meaning of a rule. Institutions are then created to impartially monitor state behavior, increase transparency and make definitive decisions about whether state actions constitute noncompliance. They facilitate cooperation through mediation, conciliation, fact-finding and binding intervention, which either prevent noncompliance from occurring or work to halt it (Abbott and Snidal 1998). As a result, regimes with such institutions produce better records of compliance than those that do not have them (Mitchell and Hensel 2007, Simmons 2000).

International institutions, however, are not always equipped with the mechanisms to detect noncompliance, often for rational reasons. Xinyuan Dai (2007) explains why international institutions have either centralized or decentralized monitoring methods. When the victims of noncompliance are primarily private groups, then decentralized monitoring regimes and NGOs or other domestic groups act as monitors or "fire alarms" to notify international organizations or other states that their government is not complying (McCubbins and Schwartz 1984).

The European Union has a legal architecture that helps monitor compliance. Article 258 empowers the Commission or individuals from a Member State or another Member State under Article 259, to notify the Commission of a suspected infringement.[3] In some situations, Preliminary References to the European Court of Justice, under Article 267, can reveal national laws that conflict with EU law. Decentralized detection methods are more effective because many of the benefits of compliance flow to private groups, while the Member States themselves have an incentive to free ride. Despite the presence of these devices to detect and enforce compliance, noncompliance still occurs in the EU. Rather than explaining why one regime performs better than another, this study accounts for why states will violate EU law in spite of effective monitoring and enforcement mechanisms.

Dai (2007) solves an important puzzle concerning how international institutions and their members design their monitoring mechanisms to enhance compliance. But her explanation focuses more on the victims than on the perpetrators of noncompliance. In many cases the language international treaties use to proscribe or prescribe certain actions enables some actors to engage in activities not covered by an agreement, though it was intended to do so. Second, when governments negotiate agreements, they often focus on the broad, long-term goals and are often unaware of the short-term costs compliance will have on *private* groups within their societies. Certainly, domestic constraints can affect the treaties between states so that these agreements are sufficiently shallow and major problems of compliance do not develop as a result (Downs *et al.* 1996).

Yet, the costs are not always known in advance to national governments or domestic groups that later will be affected by compliance. In addition, governments change their partisan make-up frequently. Right-leaning ones are sometimes more willing to tolerate some types of policy changes than left ones, and vice versa. Third, and finally, the benefits of compliance are not always concentrated nor are the costs diffused across society. The unequal distribution of costs and benefits leads to some domestic actors to mobilize against complying with international law.

Finally, if a state fails to comply, what is to be done? There are essentially two schools of thought. The enforcement school maintains that only an effective and credible form of punishment will push states into compliance. This can include targeted sanctions, programmed retaliation by other states, or exclusion from current benefits of cooperation. The management school, in contrast, sees noncompliance as the result of a government unable rather than unwilling to meet its international legal obligations (Chayes and Chayes 1995).

Instead of coercive measures, Chayes and Chayes (1995) argue that compliance must be managed, which involves both a process of clarifying the meaning of compliance and providing the resources necessary that make it possible for states to comply. Governments are oriented towards meeting their obligations under international law. They simply need to clarify what these are. Second, noncompliance is also unintentional because states realize after becoming signatories that they do not have the necessary resources to meet their legal obligations. Unaware of the problems that may develop when they negotiate an agreement, states find that they lack the technical expertise, financial or administrative resources to meet their legal obligations. Many studies of environmental accords show that regimes that possess additional resources or technical assistance generate better compliance than those that do not (Haas *et al.* 1993). Tallberg (2002) argues that compliance is so high in the EU because it possesses the tools of both schools.

The EU studies literature on noncompliance is actively testing different hypotheses for why noncompliance occurs. The management school of thought argues that difficulties in complying with EU legal demands arise because of lack of capacity and the absence of institutional ties to bring national governments and EU institutions together to discuss how best to comply. The lack of capacity among the Member States is conceptualized in various ways. They include policy or institutional misfit (Duina 1997, 1999), bureaucratic capacity (Mbaye 2001), and veto points or players (Steunenberg 2006). In these scenarios, governments wish to comply but lack the capacity to do so on time.

Other scholars of noncompliance in the EU have applied indirectly the conceptual foundations of the enforcement school. Some examine how the political preferences of those in power inhibit compliance (Treib 2003). Others have returned to examining how economic interest groups can mobilize and lobby for changes at the national level by accessing EU institutions (Grossman 2006). In so doing, these studies are indirectly assessing what the costs and benefits of complying with EU law are for the domestic groups affected. What they have not yet explained is the origin of violations of EU law and why the "losers" will mobilize their resources more often than winners to pull governments away from compliance. As a result, this study is a further extension of the approach to "bring politics back in" and examine how interest groups can delay the effects of Europeanization and other transformations of the status quo, rather than encouraging them.

Why noncompliance matters

Answering the question "why don't states comply?" will help untangle some of the puzzles that persist in both international and European politics. Admittedly, this book deals only with noncompliance in the EU. But the lessons gleaned here are applicable to other issues in international politics. Many current problems of international cooperation are infused with problems related to compliance. They include issues related to international security, political economy and other "soft issues," such as the environment, human rights and transnational criminal operations. The literature so far has identified the causes of compliance, but less so why states will fail to comply. The framework here is general enough such that the factors that inhibit compliance can be identified in these other areas of issues.

Let us take the example of nuclear nonproliferation. Some countries' efforts to acquire or spread nuclear weapons are of great concern to current foreign policy-makers and advisors. Much analysis so far focuses on why these states seek to acquire these weapons or use them as bargaining chips against the West. They also make claims about their rights under international law, such as the right to non-interference in their internal affairs. The analytical frameworks we use to understand behavior take for granted that their actions are motivated by the levels of pressure exerted by the international community, whether in terms of power or costs and benefits. They also assume that the government is a single unitary actor. However, most governments must balance their foreign policy interests against the countervailing interests of powerful domestic constituencies. And not all of these powerful groups will favor compliance. In the case of most public goods, the benefits of compliance are distributed widely across the population, but the costs are concentrated. It is the losers that are more likely to mobilize and influence their governments than the winners.

If the losers caused by compliance can be identified in advance of treaty making, then additional carrots and sticks can be inserted to limit the chances they will pressure their governments to defect. However, changes in the international balance of power, the economy, or some other exogenous shock can affect a government's compliance calculus. In addition, the inherent vagueness of the law and a regime member's inability to anticipate all of the effects of an agreement will have unintended effects that may lead to new pressures for a government not to comply. If so, then this framework will help identify the source of noncompliance and why governments may be willing to surrender to these pressures and when not.

Yet, the discussion so far assumes that states should comply. There is a growing number of scholars, lawmakers and US Supreme Court justices who argue that international law does not matter. More importantly, it has harmful effects for constitutional democracies (Rabkin 2005). This study of noncompliance is neutral in terms of whether it is normatively good for states to comply with international law. In some situations compliance with international law avoids global harms. Most people agree that international treaties related to nonproliferation of nuclear weapons, international pollution, human rights, or the trafficking of women and children are substantively positive in nature. The more states comply with their obligations to curtail these activities, the better off the rest of the world is.

But there are also important dangers or concerns related to compliance with law beyond the nation state that should not be ignored. Complying with international law can lead to conflicts between the will of the majority, produced through free and fair elections, and international institutions or law. As such, compliance with law beyond the nation state falls under the larger discussion about the rule of law versus the power of the majority to exercise its will legislatively. In particular, when international courts are perceived as overreaching when they declare some commonly accepted government activity to be noncompliant, a backlash against international institutions can ensue. My argument is decidedly neutral about where one should come down on the battle between national sovereignty and the rule of international law. Instead, my arguments seek to predict when and why violations of international law happen.

The plan of the book

In the chapters that follow, the theoretical framework for the varieties of compliance we observe in the European Union is presented. The framework here combines the insights of comparative political economy with the study of the politics of the European Union. The first part lays out the theoretical framework needed to explain noncompliance in the EU. In Chapter 2 I lay out the general hypotheses for how states navigate the countervailing pressures they face from domestic and international actors regarding compliance with international law. Chapters 3 and 4 then present two case-comparisons of noncompliance among three EU Member States. Through paired comparison in two areas related to the single European market, I show the mechanisms of domestic political pressure at work and then how international institutions responded. First, in Chapter 3, two cases of noncompliance related to the free movement of goods are discussed, specifically beer in Germany and the film industry in France. Second, in Chapter 4, two cases in the area of state aid, or unlawful government subsidies, are explored in relation to regional banks in Germany and the automobile industry in the UK. Through pairwise comparison of two similar violations in three different countries in two different policy areas, the causal mechanisms by which domestic interest groups influence national politicians can be observed.

Chapter 5 concludes by summarizing the findings of this book and the implications they have for understanding the legitimacy of international law in modern democracies. It also discusses a clear case of refusal: noncompliance with the Maastricht criteria and Stability and Growth Pact for EMU. It then turns to issues of the legitimacy of international law in democratic societies. Compliance with international law involves the interaction of different levels of governance.

It also produces serious questions about the legitimacy of international law in democratic contexts. Governments must navigate between the Scylla of possibly violating their international legal obligations and the Charybdis of ignoring the will of a majority of their citizens. National governments are held accountable to both. How they navigate those waters in the European Union is the subject of this book.

2 A theory of noncompliance

Introduction

Compliance with international law can be considered a public good. While international cooperation, arguably, makes every regime member better off, states must often deal with its costs. Those costs of compliance are frequently distributed unevenly, both at the international and the domestic level. Unless there are robust methods of assisting or punishing states for when they do not comply, the default position of a regime member is not to comply. At the domestic political level, the costs of complying are concentrated and of a high magnitude, enough for governments to choose not to change the status quo. Given the costs and predilection for noncompliance among regime members, the domestic political losers are just as likely, if not more so, to pull states away from complying as the winners push them towards it. Domestic interest groups or individuals interact with governments to shape policymakers' decisions about compliance. They not only monitor international agreements and threaten to hold governments to account, as the existing literature argues, but also pressure governments through lobbying and generating wide public support for their cause. In most cases, governments surrender when the threat of sanctions becomes credible or an independent ruling is issued. However, in some situations, international pressure will not be sufficient enough to pull states into compliance.

The theoretical framework discussed below builds on the extensive literature within the field of international relations that explores the relationship between domestic and international politics (Gourevitch 1986, Putnam 1988). Domestic politics both cause and are affected by international politics. Robert Putnam's famous "two-level game" was an apt metaphor of how the two levels interact. Jongryn Mo extended his framework into a formal game-theoretic model (Mo 1995). Assuming that the compliance or implementation phase of an agreement is different from the negotiation phase, then the preferences and even interests that states have in meeting their international legal obligations can shift over time and differently across countries. While no formal model is developed here, my argument about the types of noncompliance also suggests that the interaction of domestic and international politics produces multiple equilibria, or types of noncompliance behavior. They include full or complete compliance, inadvertent noncompliance, reluctance, and refusal, or what is termed complete noncompliance. Each of these types of compliance behavior depends on the distribution of costs and benefits at the domestic level and the degree of pressure exerted by international actors to pull governments into compliance.

This chapter sets out a rigorous but simple framework by which to understand the range of compliance behavior we can observe in the international system. The current literature in international relations is replete with examples of why states comply. There is comparatively less attention to why states do not, in spite of both enforcement and management mechanisms in place to secure it. In addition, there is an extensive body of scholarship that offers explanations for why some regimes generate better rates of compliance than others, but relatively fewer studies that explain why noncompliance varies among members of a regime. The European Union, as a highly legalized regime with both enforcement and management mechanisms to prevent noncompliance, is an excellent laboratory to answer the question as to what causes noncompliance.

In this chapter I outline the basic theoretical framework by which many problems of compliance with international law can be understood. First, I discuss how the problems of noncompliance can emerge under conditions of cooperation. Then I argue how the distribution of the costs of compliance can favor the losers over the winners. The interaction of domestic politics and international regimes produces a typology of four different types of noncompliance state behavior. This theoretical framework is then compared to some possible alternative outcomes that result from noncompliance in the European Union. Finally, studying compliance with international law is sometimes complicated by methodological difficulties. Those concerns are addressed in the conclusion to this chapter.

A theory of noncompliance

Noncompliance is a pathological phenomenon to international cooperation. Governments conclude agreements all the time. They conclude these agreements to realize the gains of cooperation, which cannot be achieved through unilateral action.[1] International treaties are made in a wide variety of areas, ranging from hindering the proliferation of nuclear weapons to the protection of women's rights. States will design international treaties and institutions with specific mechanisms, to varying degrees, to enhance their effectiveness (Koremenos *et al.* 2003). These agreements vary in specificity. For example, they vary in terms of the scope of policy areas covered, flexibility in meeting particular deadlines, and the ramifications for not meeting these deadlines (Lipson 1991). In spite of all the mechanisms and tools both states and international institutions utilize to secure the gains of cooperation, violations of and cheating on those agreements can occur often. The roots of noncompliance are in the distribution of interests in compliance at the domestic level.

Compliance with international law can be considered a public good. While international cooperation, arguably, makes every regime member better off, states must often deal with its costs. Those costs of compliance are frequently distributed unevenly, both at the international and domestic level. Unless there are robust methods of assisting or punishing states when they do not comply, the default position of a regime member is not to comply. At the domestic political level, the costs of complying are concentrated and of a high magnitude, enough so that governments choose not to change the status quo. Given the costs and predilection for noncompliance among regime members, the domestic political losers are just as likely, if not more so, to pull states away from complying as the winners push them towards it. Domestic interest groups or individuals interact with governments to shape policymakers' decisions about compliance. They not only monitor international agreements and threaten to hold governments to account, as the existing literature argues, but also pressure governments through lobbying and generating wide public support for their cause. In most cases, governments surrender when the threat of sanctions becomes credible or an independent ruling is issued. However, in some situations, international pressure will not be sufficient enough to pull states into compliance as a result of either concentrated costs of a very high magnitude.

According to the liberal theory of international relations, state preferences for an agreement are the result of domestic factors, such as government policy preferences and powerful interests groups, and how they are aggregated at the national level (Moravcsik 1997). States then bargain with others in light of these preferences and the agreement reached represents the lowest common denominator for policy change among them (Moravcsik 1991, 1993). The resulting agreements then vary in the extent to which they demand their members to make changes to the status quo. It is possible to imagine then some agreements that will require few changes, at least for those members who can hold out the longest and gain least from the proposed agreement. Thus, there may be some circumstances in which the agreements made by states require little change to the status quo (Downs 1998, Downs *et al.* 1996). Noncompliance is not likely to occur if the agreements they are making are shallow.

Yet the liberal theory of international relations stops at the negotiating table. Even in the case of shallow agreements, noncompliance can occur. Dai lays out several reasons why the implementation phase is different from the bargaining phase. The costs of compliance are only observed after the agreement has been concluded. Mobilization by groups seeking compliance or noncompliance often takes place only after the treaty is concluded (Dai 2005: 375). I extend her analysis by identifying essentially four different reasons why noncompliance is a common occurrence.

There are many reasons why noncompliance, even in the strongest international regimes, will occur. First, all regime members have a status quo bias. They would prefer not to make changes to the status quo and simply accrue the benefits of cooperation. And if all other states can also do so, then cooperation is a non-zero sum game and mutually beneficial. But if the agreement calls for only small changes to the status quo that lower transaction costs, increase reliability, or provide economic or political gains that cannot be achieved without cooperation, then states will often construct and comply with those agreements. As a result, some scholars suggest international law does nothing more than reflect state interests (Goldsmith and Posner 2005). However, the likelihood that a vast majority of international agreements and legal obligations produce perfect or near-perfect congruence between a country's legal obligation and its interests is not very high. And states still have the incentive to free ride. Noncompliance is hard to detect. Each state has the incentive to defect and yet enjoy the benefits of cooperation. No state wants to risk the costs of retaliation, especially if the threat is credible. As a result, there is always a bias in favor of defection. Thus, noncompliance is likely to be a common occurrence.

Governments construct agreements or abide by international law because it makes the state or its own powerful constituencies better off. They would not have agreed to cooperate if they felt credibly threatened by the possible domestic losers associated with an agreement and, consequently, would experience some electoral or other political losses associated with the agreement. At the bargaining stage, governments are often more or at least as concerned about the total benefits available for the country as a whole as for their own constituents. Policymakers have both private and public reasons for the decisions they make. While their motivations are mixed, they are just as likely to be making these agreements for the general welfare of the country as for their own private benefit or for the benefit of powerful domestic constituencies, especially if increased cooperation is likely in the future.

During the negotiation phase, governments must play a complex two-level game and make a series of trade-offs. They must reach a deal that considers the costs and benefits of cooperation at the international level, a country's status or gains *vis-à-vis* other countries, compared to the possible costs and benefits at the domestic level. Hypothetically, governments construct regimes to make every regime member better off, while ignoring or discounting the domestic costs of those agreements. Those gains may be significant for the country as a whole because the agreement lays down the groundwork for future cooperation, prevents immediate or near-term threats or harms from developing, or simply strengthens the whole region or international community. Gains and losses are also measured in terms of the relative or absolute position of a country *vis-à-vis* other members for the country as a whole.[2] Often there is not a one-to-one relationship between domestic costs and benefits and those secured at the international level for the country as a whole.

If states are choosing to cooperate, the domestic political gains should be at least equal to if not greater than the losses for the country as a whole. But they may not be evenly distributed among various groups at home. Furthermore, as the preferences of states at the negotiating table are aggregated and the national interest is formed, some groups are more represented than others. Some have more political access than others. Once bargaining takes places, policymakers often choose to make some sacrifices in order to secure other gains. Those benefits and costs are not distributed evenly across countries or within them. Thus, governments are often willing to sacrifice the present or future domestic costs of an agreement for the international gains of the present or future.

While true, the losers who feared the adoption of the new international rule do not disappear. If there are costs associated with international cooperation, they are likely borne by the groups or individuals who did not support cooperation, and were either excluded from the negotiation phase or governments chose to ignore or discount them.

Second, governments often conclude agreements under conditions of uncertainty. Governments cannot anticipate all of the possible costs associated with the agreement. However, they rarely leave an institutional regime or defect from an agreement. They defect from the regime only if those costs become prohibitively large. In addition, not all of the unintended consequences of an international rule are necessarily harmful. States can also enjoy unanticipated benefits. My argument is only that these unintended costs occur at least as often as the benefits. Even if they do not, the losses associated with unintended consequences usually are concentrated among a small group, while some groups or even the country as a whole enjoy the benefits. For example, if an independent body responsible for dispute resolution is created, such as an international court, then the process of litigation can lead to further refinement in the meaning of the law and thus produce unintended effects for its members in the form of new legal obligations. Alec Stone Sweet's studies of how the legal process in the European Union constructed a supranational order serve as an excellent example (Stone Sweet 2000, 2004). Not only did the process of interaction generate greater authority for the ECJ and construct a supranational polity, the prescriptions and proscriptions associated with an international rule also became more specific over time.

Cases of noncompliance are likely to grow until either the law becomes stable or states learn to fully comply. The extent to which the law is unstable and state behavior must change over time depends on the size of the "compliance gap (Downs and Trento 2004)." There is almost always enough ambiguity in law itself to generate some amount of noncompliance. Since my theoretical framework is intended to explain cross-national variation within a regime, and not total noncompliance, whether this gap is large or small or changes over time should not affect the distribution of legal violations. For example, in the European Union, EU law can be characterized as an evolving process that filled gaps over time in terms of how the law should be interpreted and applied.[3] But this book addresses less how much of a compliance gap exists in the EU and is more directed towards understanding the asymmetrical effects the gap has on EU Member States. If the law is becoming more stable over time and further specifying what state practices are allowed or prohibited, then the sources of those violations are also revealing the actors and interests that oppose those changes.

The evolution of EU law in the area of the free movement of goods shows how the flexibility in the law eventually narrows the scope of activities allowed by the EC Treaty. The EC Treaty of 1963 contains two important articles related to the free movement of goods within the European Community. Articles 34 and 35 prohibit quantitative restrictions and measures of equivalent effect on imports and exports, respectively. However, Article 36 stipulates that restrictions on trade in goods based on grounds of public morality, public policy or security are permitted. Years of EU legal jurisprudence were needed to determine which policies were perceived as legitimate, which policy methods of achieving those goals were permitted, and what authority the Commission and European Court of Justice have to enforce these provisions (Maduro 1998). Restrictions on the free movement of goods were gradually lifted throughout the EU, and the authority of the European Court of Justice (ECJ) and Commission would grow in scope (Stone Sweet 2004, Stone Sweet and Brunnel 1998). These restrictions did not just cover tariffs, but also qualitative restrictions that affected intra-European trade. This included selling arrangements, product contents and licensing procedures. As legalization in the European Union increased, ambiguity and flexibility in the law decreased. In addition, governments increasingly adapted their policies to meet their EU legal requirements. Yet, as explained below, the law is not so unstable that the sources of noncompliance cannot be identified a priori.

Another reason for uncertainty about the future costs and benefits of an agreement is that there are often significant levels of flexibility within an international regulation that can also lead to unintended consequences for a regime's members. States build flexibility into their agreements to ease the process of changing the status quo, generate wider agreement, and allow for some adaptation to change over time (Abbott 2000, Lipson 1991). But there are limits to any level of flexibility. As levels of flexibility in the law increase, its precision decreases. As precision decreases, it becomes more uncertain and improbable that the goal of international cooperation will be fulfilled. The greater degree of flexibility that states have in terms of defining what practices satisfy some legal requirement, what methods are appropriate to satisfy it, and the timeline allowed to satisfy it, the more likely the purposes of cooperation are not reached. As Downs *et al.* (1996) would conclude, if the agreement is so flexible that it is quite "shallow," then compliance is occurring because so little is required of the state to change the status quo. Thus, states are always seeking a balance between flexibility and precision.

Conversely, the more precise an international agreement is, the more likely noncompliance will occur, controlling for the "depth" of the agreement. If there are lower levels of flexibility, then governments have less leeway in maintaining the status quo. Less flexibility in the law means that governments know in advance what policies must be implemented or terminated. Less flexibility also means there is more precision in terms of what methods are appropriate for complying with the rule. The amount of time granted to comply with an international rule also becomes clearer. Again, this assumes that there is some compliance gap. Therefore, as flexibility decreases, the probability of noncompliance increases.

Third, and finally, noncompliance occurs for reasons exogenous to the international agreement or law. After an agreement on a new international rule is reached, the domestic political conditions that enabled it can change or break down. New political coalitions form with different positions on the Left–Right ideological spectrum. Political regimes can also become more or less democratic over time. A government's interest in the agreement can also change over time as legal interpretations of the treaty change. The relative power of an interest group, which either supports or opposes compliance with international law, can wane and wax over time. As economic or social changes occur, different domestic groups become politically salient. For example, new social movements develop, or interest groups find new ways to organize and influence governments to affect compliance behavior. The establishment of a new treaty can also create or strengthen groups in favor of compliance and weaken those who are not.

To summarize, international agreements often produce losers. They are the actors that fail to have their preferences aggregated at the international level during bargaining. Uncertainty and flexibility, as well as the inherent vagueness of law and language, lead to unintended consequences that harm their interests. Third, exogenous changes transform state interests over time. These factors serve as the conditions for noncompliance.

States commit instances of noncompliance all the time. They are also frequently likely to be brought into compliance under some conditions. Unless the case of noncompliance is particularly severe and extremely harmful to a state's interests, particularly over the long term, enforcement and management measures are weak, or the agreement is sufficiently flexible, states will eventually choose to comply with an international regime's or its members' demands. The puzzle that remains to be explained is why governments behave differently when violations do happen. In some cases, governments will change the status quo immediately when discovering the violation. In other situations, the government will delay compliance until an international court makes an official ruling. Noncompliance not only occurs often, but the interests of domestic groups who oppose changes to the status quo also drive it. The interaction of the losers and international pressure to effect compliance produces a variety of noncompliance behavior.

Noncompliance as a two-level game

The discussion above explains why noncompliance, theoretically, is a significant problem in the international system. How much noncompliance there is within a particular international regime is a task for empirical research. Next, I turn to the possible causes of noncompliance and why different types of noncompliance behavior occur.

States fail to meet their obligations under international law because of the problems of collective action. They attempt to enjoy the benefits of international cooperation while avoiding its costs. Assume that a regime member concluded the agreement to make it better off. We must also assume that international agreement, after bargaining with other members, required some amount of change to the status quo. If the agreement does require substantial changes, then the agreement produced both *costs* and benefits for the member. Those costs are more likely to be concentrated, while the benefits are diffused across society.

In many cases the gains governments seek through international cooperation qualify as public goods.[4] The types of public goods produced by agreements vary. They range from military alliances to combat state and non-state security threats to agreements and guidelines over the movement of financial instruments, such as the Basel Accords. They also vary in specificity. The Interim Agreement between the EU and the US over terrorist financing was specific in what types of data could be collected regarding financial transfers. In contrast, the recent Copenhagen Accord of December 2009 only established a vague set of goals to mitigate the causes and effects of global climate change. Although these agreements vary in type and specificity, they seek to provide important international public goods. As a result, however, they are also all susceptible to the problems of collective action.

To qualify as a public good, the good must be nonrival and nonexclusive. A public good is nonrival when its consumption by one member to the agreement does not the ability of others to consume it. A public good is nonexclusive when consumers of the good cannot be excluded from its consumption at low cost to other members (Olson 1965). Extensive free riding can occur as a result. Since every member's dominant strategy is to free ride, the collective good is not produced unless the agreements the members devise contain elements that prevent cheating. These measures include methods to increase transparency to detect cheating, side-payments or policy linkages to generate private gains, or promises of future gains over the long term if cooperation is successful (Keohane 1984).

Is European integration an example of a public good? Some of the gains of cooperation accrue only when a state has EU membership. The ability for agreements to be enforced under EU law, address problems of market failure, and establish EU-wide agreements with third parties, reduces transaction costs, but benefits only EU members. Non-members do enjoy the indirect benefits of growing national economies and higher levels of trade as integration deepens and widens. But within the EU, once membership is obtained, most of the gains can be enjoyed without having to contribute until financial payments became mandatory and cheating was monitored. At the same time, Member States enjoy specific private benefits. These can include strengthening of a country's export sector, larger markets for its agricultural goods, and financial or development assistance for poor regions of the country, such as the EU's Structural and Cohesion funds. As a result, because European integration results in both public and private gains, it is more of an impure public good or "joint product model."

One additional way in which the EU produces a public good is that a Member State could rationally defect from an agreement, often with little risk of retaliation or punishment. Furthermore, one Member State's consumption of the public good would not affect another's consumption. The varying levels of interest and size among the members belonging to an agreement or institution also creates problems for providing the public good and international cooperation. Some members will benefit more than others and thus more strongly prefer the production of the public good. Similarly, some members are more able than others to produce the public good. In the case of hegemony, one state in the international system is willing and capable of providing the public good because the gains of cooperation exceed the costs of its providing it, while others will enjoy it without contributing. But in most regimes, these types of inequality also need addressing if cooperation is to succeed. As long as the private gains to the largest member exceed the relative cost of its provision, the public good is produced. In this scenario, the small exploit the large.

Level one: the domestic politics of noncompliance

While the impure public good model best describes the results of European integration at the domestic level, economic integration is a pure public good for the country as a whole. At the domestic level, everyone enjoys the benefits of European integration. Yet few have the incentive to produce it themselves. Whether re-entry into the community of nations or enlarging markets for French agricultural goods, each individual German or French farmer would enjoy these benefits irrespective of whether they worked to support compliance or not. The gains of cooperation are distributed unevenly across the national population, as are the costs. The relative motivation levels of different groups to produce an agreement also vary as a result. In some cases, governments secure side-payments for the losers. But the losers are sometimes ignored if they are an unimportant constituency or the government cannot secure such a deal for them when bargaining with other countries. There are also winners produced by an agreement, who either supported its creation or find new avenues to achieve their policy objectives. But the gains of cooperation are often diffused across a large population, while the costs are concentrated. The question to answer is whether the losers are more likely to pull countries away from compliance than the winners will push them towards it.

My approach for explaining both the origins of noncompliance and the resulting types of behavior builds on Xinyuan Dai's model of the domestic compliance mechanisms (Dai 2007). Dai explains why compliance occurs even when institutional mechanisms for monitoring are weak and signatories have an incentive to shirk. In brief, she develops a game-theoretic model that shows how domestic constituents, the winners, can push policymakers into compliance or notify international institutions that noncompliance is taking place. Dai argues that domestic constituencies in support of an agreement can push policymakers into complying by exerting electoral pressure under certain conditions. Acting as "fire alarms," domestic constituents use electoral pressure to persuade elected policymakers that compliance is both in their public and private interests. The power of domestic constituents depends on their level of information, the ability to detect noncompliance, and the degree to which the state is centralized. When domestic constituents are not strongly organized and unable to exert electoral pressure or without information, they are unlikely to be effective. In Dai's formulation, the victims of noncompliance help overcome problems of collective action and the provision of the international public good.

One of the important insights of Xinyuan Dai's model is how domestic political constituencies, assuming a certain level of information and strength, can push otherwise ambivalent policymakers to comply with international law. Domestic groups help overcome the collective action problems associated with international agreements. Small groups are more likely to be able to monitor an agreement than large ones, unless the latter have equal or more levels of information than the former. Her model and empirical cases studies, however, appear to focus on the relative strength of the victims of defection to monitor compliance compared to those who oppose it. For example, she argues that compliance with the 1985 Sulfur Protocol varied among European countries according to the strength of domestic environmental groups and public opinion in favor of protecting the environment (Dai 2007: 84–99).[5] Because of this variation in the strength of domestic environmental movements, there were different levels of compliance with the Protocol. Yet, Dai appears to be limiting her discussion to how the victims of noncompliance influence policymakers and is missing the power of the perpetrators.[6]

The questions Dai's model raises are several-fold. Do perpetrators prevent noncompliance more often than victims push for compliance? Next, if they do, which mechanisms enhance the ability of small groups to influence policymakers, besides electoral pressure? Similarly, Beth Simmons points to how compliance is improved and international law matters through executive agenda setting, litigation and social mobilization (Simmons 2009). Are losers or winners more likely to use these mechanisms to push through their agendas? Finally, can we always assume that the general public will be in favor of complying? I argue that the losers are just as likely to use these mechanisms to stop compliance as the winners, if not more so.

The losers associated with complying with international law are likely to be more successful in pulling policymakers away from complying than the victims of noncompliance will push them towards it, because these costs are sometimes concentrated and mainly affect small groups. The changes to the status quo are likely to affect a small number of individuals or groups. In contrast, the benefits of cooperation are spread or diffused across society. In such situations, the losers related to compliance are more motivated to lobby their governments than the winners. The costs of mobilizing, obtaining information and pressuring their representatives to maintain the status quo are likely to be less than the costs to them if the government complies with the international rule. In contrast, the benefits of continued compliance are distributed across the population, which implies that they have less incentive to mobilize to lobby in favor of continued compliance.[7]

In order to generate political mobilization against complying, the costs must exceed a minimal threshold for these domestic groups. Even if domestic actors have a strong interest in complying, they will not mobilize resources to fight compliance in all situations in which they have a great interest in the outcome. Thus, not only must the costs of compliance be concentrated, they must reach a significant threshold to motivate political action. The magnitude of the costs can be independent of the size of the group. For example, if there is a ban against genocide and a government or militia leader is accused of committing war atrocities, then that individual faces trial and punishment. The costs are highly concentrated and of a high magnitude for the individual, but relatively low for all of society.[8] The benefits of bringing the war criminal to justice may be high for society at large, but, with the exception perhaps of the victims of human rights abuses themselves, those benefits are diffuse across society. Because every member is likely to benefit from justice rendered irrespective of whether they contribute to the political fight to bring the war criminal to justice, they are more likely to free ride. And the victims can free ride on those groups litigating or mobilizing to obtain compliance. In contrast, the losers associated with compliance will experience severe private losses if a government complies.

Monitoring and encouraging governments to comply by domestic actors is also not without its political, economic and social costs. Winners associated with state compliance can face political obstacles and resource constraints that the losers do not. For example, if human rights activists and victims of genocide wish to hold the perpetrators to account, they will often confront opposition from their own government. If they do experience benefits from compliance, those gains can sometimes occur long into the future; for example, if a war criminal is transported to an international court for trial, a conviction is not likely to be swift or certain. Thus, domestic groups of a variety of sorts face uncertain chances of success and comparatively higher levels of the risk of harm, at least in the case of human rights. This is not to argue that domestic interest groups do not succeed in securing compliance. But, what is often ignored is that war criminals are just as, if not more, concerned about possible prosecution than the human rights activists and victims of genocide are interested in seeing them tried and convicted before an international court. The perpetrators face the risk of trial, conviction and punishment. Given the risks and costs the beneficiaries of compliance face compared to those who lose from noncompliance, on balance, a state's default position is not to comply.

Why then would we expect losers to mobilize more often and effectively than the winners? First, governments usually have a status quo bias. After all, the prime motivation for defection, which beneficiaries should be monitoring, is to maintain the status quo while enjoying the benefits of cooperation, assuming the benefits constitute a public good. Moreover, the government may only have signed the treaty to signal it wishes to cooperate in the future, but not this time. This assumes, again, that compliance has some costly elements or that some "gap" exists.

Second, powerful domestic constituencies in favor of maintaining the status quo already exist. They often shaped the bargaining calculus for governments as they negotiated the terms of an international agreement. Therefore, if unintended consequences related to the agreement develop that are averse to their interests, they will most likely experience their impact. Losers associated with an agreement are likely to have more intense objections to compliance than other groups favoring compliance, and noncompliance will be more common than compliance.

Losers can also achieve political influence on par or even with the winners. In many circumstances, they prevent compliance through the same methods as used by the winners. As Dai demonstrates, both interest groups and the population at large can monitor conditions on the ground and use electoral pressure to push governments into compliance. For example, under Article 258, individuals from a Member State in which the violation is occurring, or a private person or firm in another Member State who feels harmed, can notify the Commission of the suspected violation. But the losers are just as likely to use these mechanisms to prevent compliance. They also have strong incentives to monitor international legal developments. The costs of complying with a treaty are more likely to be concentrated among them than the winners. When international regimes have decentralized regimes, they can become the target of noncompliant behavior.

A third reason why losers will mobilize is that international institutions are more interested in prosecuting the offenders than rewarding the compliant. Because institutions can use prosecutions of members to expand their authority and widen the scope of their missions, they often seek to prosecute the offenders, whether states or individuals. Since each member government has an incentive to free ride on the agreement, they have some incentive to report others for shirking their legal duties. However, since reporting noncompliance by others can lead to retaliatory behavior by other regime members, and cases of noncompliance are often hard to detect, they must weigh their decision to set off the fire alarm against the possibility of others finding their own code violations. International institutions, such as the UN, can also create domestic allies within countries to help detect when their own governments are violating a country's international legal obligations (Simmons 2009). But just as there are transnational activists (Keck and Sikkink 1998) or communities of legal scholars and judges (Slaughter 2004) that work with each other and international institutions to secure compliance, there are also transnational organizations, such as multinational corporations, crime syndicates, narcotraffickers and international terrorist groups that work to prevent state compliance. Therefore, the question is no longer how transnational actors enhance compliance with international law, but which types of transnational actors, "bad" or "good," are more powerful and under what conditions.

Legalization makes the losers more sensitive to change than the winners. As legalization of the agreement increases, the range of accepted state behavior is more likely to narrow than to expand. As international courts issue additional rulings, case law develops and uncertainty or imprecision in the law decreases, which can limit the amount of accepted legal behavior. This is not true in all cases. In the case of the legal doctrine of the free movement of goods, discussed in Chapter 3, an expansive notion of what state regulatory practices constituted violations of EU law was later narrowed in the face of growing Member State opposition.

Domestic constituencies can generate opposition to complying with an international rule as much as others try to gain support for compliance within the general population. When an international institution calls for the elimination of environmental regulations, job protections, or subsidies for an industry that are perceived as part of a national tradition, popular support for noncompliance can emerge. This was the case concerning the Beer Purity Law in Germany. Because domestic brewers in Bavaria and other parts of Germany could frame the Commission's calls for reform in the *Reinheitsgebot* as a threat to national traditions, popular sentiment against compliance grew over time. This was a contributing factor to the German government's decision to delay compliance until the ECJ issued a decisive ruling, and even fail to fully comply until there was additional litigation. Opposition to the role of international law in domestic society, as expressed by national judges, legal cultures and tradition, or by even domestic society in general, can also slow or even prevent compliance.[9] If the population at large perceives neither international institutions nor international law, in general, as legitimate, then noncompliance is also likely to happen.

In conclusion, there are powerful incentives for governments to defect from the agreements they make. If the costs of complying are concentrated and of a high magnitude, domestic actors will pressure governments not to comply. But, governments do not choose to comply or not based solely on the basis of the relative power of interest groups. They must also weigh their policy decisions against the costs and benefits at the international level.

Level two: the international politics of noncompliance

Policymakers do not choose to comply or not in an international vacuum. They must also weigh the costs and benefits of complying in light of incentives and disincentives at the international level. International institutions and less formalized regimes possess a variety of tools to maintain compliance. They can both give out carrots and wave their sticks to bring countries into compliance. Carrots come in the form of financial or technological assistance when noncompliance would result from insufficient government capacity. They can serve as side-payments to groups harmed by changes to the status quo. In contrast, sticks come in the form of sanctions, retaliation or, in extreme circumstances, expulsion from the regime. In these circumstances, states are forgoing not only the benefits of cooperation generated by the agreement, but also possible future gains.

Yet governments must ultimately choose between compliance and noncompliance, or find some way of renegotiating the nature of their international legal obligation. In light of domestic pressures to maintain the status quo and yet also meet their international legal obligations, policymakers must navigate a difficult political dilemma. One solution is for them to delay complying until either an international court issues a definitive ruling or an international consensus emerges that the suspected behavior constitutes noncompliance. When governments rely on international courts issuing a ruling against a government, national leaders often use these rulings as justifications to their domestic constituents for saying why changes to the status quo must be made, irrespective of their concerns. In the case of the European Union, the "blame Brussels or Luxembourg" effect is a common occurrence, whereby national policymakers cite their international legal obligations as reasons why they must make unpopular changes to the status quo (Smith 1997). After an independent arbiter has made a ruling and it is against the interests of the state not to comply, then an institution or state can initiate a subsequent stage that carries far more risk for a country. The application of sanctions, retaliation and other forms of punishment increases in probability. In addition, governments no longer want to sacrifice the short-term gains of satisfying a powerful domestic constituency for the long-term benefits of international cooperation. International courts and their rulings can act as powerful agents that legitimize and help justify changes needed to the status quo.

If an international regime does not have an independent arbiter, then compliance is determined once consensus is reached among regime members that the offending practice does not quite qualify as noncompliance. They can also begin proceedings to punish the country in the form of sanctions, retaliation or exclusion from sharing the public good. Yet, as proponents of the legalization school would argue, achieving consensus among regime members, in terms of whether the suspect behavior is noncompliance and what is to be done, is more difficult than when an independent arbiter exists. Therefore, enforcement becomes weaker the less legalized an international institution is. As the threats of punishment become less credible, noncompliant behavior is likely to continue. Thus, less institutionalized and legalized regimes experience more noncompliance (Zürn and Joerges 2005). However, the effectiveness of international courts to shift state behavior is conditioned by the relative legitimacy of both the court's ruling and the authority that the institution itself has in national society. Therefore, highly legalized regimes will not always perform better in terms of securing compliance than those that are less legalized.

Given these options, governments face difficult political choices. From the bottom, they face strong political pressure not to comply. When the costs of compliance are high but concentrated, governments will delay their decision to comply. When the costs of compliance are also high for the country as a whole, especially over the long term, they are less likely to change their behavior. Moreover, when there are not sufficient levels of legalization, punishment mechanisms or forms of assistance, then the likelihood grows that a regime member will remain noncompliant. When an international regime has sufficient levels of legitimacy, or its collective ruling is perceived as such, compliance becomes more likely. The interaction of these countervailing pressures produces a variety of compliance behaviors.

Types of noncompliance

The interaction of the magnitude of the compliance costs and whether they are concentrated or diffused, along with the strength of the international regime, produces four different types of government response. First, governments may be complying already with the agreements they made, or will quickly do so in order to realize the gains of cooperation. Existing compliance, or the absence of noncompliance, is occurring for at least two reasons. First, the agreement did not require any changes to the status quo, or the required changes to the status quo were so minimal that no problems of noncompliance would emerge. Another possibility is that the regime member was able to fully anticipate the expected costs of compliance and either prepared domestic compensation measures for the losers, or discounted their possible negative impact in the future.

In the second type of compliance behavior, the costs of complying are concentrated but are of a low magnitude. In this scenario, a gap between the goals or purpose of the international agreement and existing state practices is discovered. These cases generally involve small, technical matters and arise because of the unintended consequences of the rule. But this does not imply that the costs are not concentrated. While the national regulation suspected of infringing an international agreement may appear to be an issue of relative minutiae, it can have important effects on the manufacturing or marketing of products or services for a single or several firms within a specific economic sector. However, although the costs of complying are concentrated among small groups, since they are of a relatively low magnitude these firms or interest groups choose not to mobilize to prevent changes to the status quo. In addition, large amounts of political, economic or social pressure are brought to bear on a country by the international community or an institution.

In a third scenario of noncompliance behavior, the costs of complying are concentrated and of a great magnitude. In these circumstances, interest groups and firms are likely to mobilize their political resources to prevent the government from complying. As a result, the process of complying is delayed and fraught with legal battles. If a neutral arbiter exists, such as an international court, then compliance will not occur until a final ruling is made. If no neutral arbiter exists and the international regime is less institutionalized, then the threats of punishment occur once some type of international consensus emerges that the suspect state behavior qualifies as noncompliance, although not in all cases. Economic sanctions, financial aid or legal clarifications can help states become compliant. In this scenario as well, a strong, highly legalized institution, or successful international coordinated action, might be necessary to generate compliance. With a sufficient amount of financial or political pressure, governments will sacrifice the short-term costs of compliance in light of the larger, credible costs imposed by foreign actors, or for the long-term gains of increased cooperation.

Even after the court's ruling or when international consensus is reached, noncompliance can continue as the government attempts to evade the ramifications of its decision. While the chief concern of the international court or enforcing institution is addressed, new revisions or versions of the law can cause continued noncompliance as governments find methods of retaining the status quo while satisfying their international legal obligations. Governments are likely to refrain from this practice until the costs of maintaining the status quo exceed the domestic benefits, usually for the country at large. These costs can come in the form of sanctions by the international regime, retaliation by other members, or damages to its reputation. Governments are risking the loss of future gains of cooperation while also attempting to satisfy the demands of powerful constituents. In most cases, a regime member will eventually choose to comply as the costs of defection increase in magnitude and probability when the international regime has the tools to create compliance.

The fourth and final form of noncompliance, refusal, describes the situation when the costs of compliance outweigh its benefits for a country as a whole. In this scenario, the costs of compliance are either concentrated or diffused across society, but are of a sufficiently high magnitude that governments choose not to comply. They can also be long-term in nature. The costs of complying can arise either because of domestic interest groups exerting so much pressure on incumbent governments not to comply or because the costs for the country as a whole are perceived as too high. A government's decision to remain in complete noncompliance can also be a function of the probability that sanctions will be imposed or other members will retaliate. When the probability of additional punishment is low, governments have even more incentive to defect completely from their international legal obligations. The government is also choosing to sacrifice the possibility of future long-term cooperation for immediate short-term benefits. Table 2.1 summarizes the type of noncompliance behavior that developed as a result of the interaction between the types of compliance costs and their magnitude.

These types of compliance behavior occur irrespective of whether the cause of noncompliance is unwillingness or incapacity. According to the enforcement school, discussed in Chapter 1, noncompliance occurs in the absence of effective punishment or other enforcement mechanisms to change state behavior and prevent cheating or defection. The types of compliance behavior outlined above show how domestic costs interact with a compliance regime that has enforcement mechanisms. Some scholars argue that enforcement is a necessary and sufficient condition for compliance. I argue instead that the effectiveness of an enforcement mechanism depends on the cost–benefit calculus a government makes as it compares the costs of complying with the benefits of not complying at the domestic level. Why some states fail to comply more often than others is a function of the costs every country is experiencing, but to different degrees. If we observe that governments are often complying with regimes that have effective

Table 2.1 Types of noncompliance

	Short-term losses concentrated	*Long-term losses concentrated*
Low Magnitude of Costs	Accommodation	Obedience
High Magnitude of Costs	Reluctance	Refusal
	Strong International Regime or Institutions	*Weak international Regime or Institutions*

enforcement mechanisms, this means they compare the costs of defection against the benefits of complying, and the latter exceeds the former. If the benefits of cooperation constitute a club good, then simple exclusion from enjoying the benefits of cooperation could prevent defection.

Similarly, if a government is failing to comply because of problems of incapacity, then this typology of noncompliance also applies and helps to predict state behavior. First, cases of inadvertent noncompliance can occur if there are disagreements over the meaning of an international rule or its application. The costs of transposing the status quo may be concentrated, but not of such a magnitude that domestic groups or the state will balk from complying. Second, if the costs of complying are of a significant magnitude because of a lack of technological or financial resources, then noncompliance is likely to occur until sufficient assistance is provided. If additional assistance is not provided or a country is still unable to fulfill its international legal obligations due to insufficient resources, then complete noncompliance, or refusal, is likely to result.

The theoretical framework is also applicable to situations in which the causes of noncompliance are ideational or normative in character. Cases of noncompliance will not emerge if societal actors and governments perceive both the international regime and the rule it is pronouncing as legitimate or appropriate. Inadvertent noncompliance can happen when there is discordance, or "misfit," between the domestic norm and the international rule. As Abram and Antonia Chayes suggest, legal discourse between the two parties can assist in resolving the dispute (Chayes and Chayes 1995, Chayes *et al.* 1998, see also Koh 1996, 1997, Kratochwil 1989). This does not imply that domestic interest groups do not mobilize around the suspected legal infringement by their government. If the dispute over the international rule is over contested normative proscriptions, groups can be opposed to its application. However, they will not mobilize significant resources to prevent compliance. Third, if the magnitude of difference between the national and international norm is large, then reluctant compliance is likely to occur. Domestic interest groups, perceiving the gap between the international norm and national practice as large, can mobilize to prevent compliance. Compliance will occur only when an independent court issues a decisive ruling on the matter or a new form of international consensus emerges. Finally, complete noncompliance, or refusal, is likely to happen when domestic groups and the incumbent government perceive both the norm and the institution as illegitimate, such as bans on the use of land mines or torture of prisoners of war.

The comprehensive framework presented here tracks closely with Clifford Carrubba's work on compliance and international courts, particularly within the context of Member State behavior under the rule of the European Court of Justice (Carrubba 2005). First, similar to my argument, Carrubba (2005) doubts that other governments can perfectly control defection by other Member States, or even would want to. I argue as well that, contrary to Downs *et al.* (1996), some agreements are not shallow and will require changes to the status quo that are materially significant (ibid.: 670). Carrubba then develops a formal model in which he identifies the sequence of interaction between the Court and a Member

State that reflects the theoretical framework here. At its termination, a regime member faces the choice of whether to ignore a Court's ruling of noncompliance and risk punishment by other members or maintain the status quo (ibid.: 672–676). Carrubba's analysis leads to several key conclusions. Among them is that regime members are not likely to comply when the costs of doing so are high. Since international courts know this, they are not likely to issue adverse rulings. Members will comply with a court's ruling only when the costs of doing so are low compared to the likelihood of punishment, which depends on the willingness of other regime members to punish the defector (ibid.: 677).

My theoretical framework both extends but also questions Carrubba's conclusions. First, using standard theories of political economy, I identify what costs members are "drawing" and when they are small and when they are large. Low costs of compliance depend on whether the costs of compliance are concentrated or diffuse and whether they are of a high magnitude or low. Those costs are a function of the winners and losers produced by the EC Treaty and whether the domestic losers mobilize to prevent the country from immediately complying.

Yet, according to Carrubba, the primary reason a country complies with a court ruling is the belief that other countries will retaliate. There are several problems with this argument. First, the threat of retaliation is not credible. If other Member States punished a defecting state, their own violations would come to light. Second, we observe little retaliation over the history of the EU. Member States rarely use Article 259 to notify the Commission of noncompliant behavior by another member. For Carrubba to be correct that regime members comply often, even in low-cost situations, it must be because they fear retaliation in many situations. We neither observe that in the case of the EU nor would realistically expect it. After all, it would be very costly for Member States to constantly threaten another Member State for noncompliant behavior in every instance, even when the Court identifies its precise nature. Talk is not cheap. In a regime where hundreds of cases of possible noncompliance are discovered each year, and 90 percent of the time the defending government loses, threats of retaliation are not likely to be the tool of compliance.

Finally, the rationalist approach Carrubba employs is derived from the realist school of international relations. He argues that compliance with ECJ ruling is more a function of the threat of retaliation by other countries than it is a reflection of the independent power of the Court. Underlying Carrubba's analysis is an assumption that, in an anarchic system, only the actions of other states and their threats of punishment to change the rational calculus of the defecting member can change its behavior. In short, there is little room for the independent power of international courts and law itself (Carr 1964, Hoffmann 1956, Morganthau 1951). However, in the European Union and elsewhere, we observe that countries comply with court rulings in high-cost situations even when the threat of retaliation is absent or the ruling is a victory for a weaker power, because a country feels a sense of obligation to obey the law (Alter 2008, Bull 1977, Reus-Smit 2004). Even at the state level, both powerful individuals and branches of government will obey adverse court rulings when the ruling is fundamentally against their interests. There is evidence that both domestic and international courts do fear to tread on the powers of legislatures or presidencies (Harvey and Friedman 2006, Vanberg 2005, Staton 2006). There are many important cases when other branches of government choose to comply because it is appropriate in a society governed by the rule of law, such as *Bush v. Gore* and *Hamdan v. Rumsfeld*.[10] Thus, despite President Jackson's famous quip, "John Marshall [the US Supreme Court] has made its ruling, now let him enforce it,"[11] courts rarely have to employ the long arm of the law to achieve compliance by other branches of government. This does not mean that courts are not political institutions and do not fear retaliation by other political institutions or actors if they make rulings that challenge their interests and, therefore, preemptively restrict the impact of their rulings on them. But when, under what conditions and how often are all empirical questions. Lastly, international regimes and institutions vary in their ability to sanction noncompliance, reward or bring states into compliance. Thus, we should expect the role of retaliation and raw power moves to generate compliance also to vary across institutions or regimes.

So far I have outlined the basic theoretical framework for why noncompliance is likely to happen and why it happens more often than compliance. Because governments prefer to maintain the status quo, free riding, and do not want to risk the wrath of powerful domestic constituencies dependent on the status quo, they will delay compliance. But governments must weigh the benefits of pleasing an important interest group against the costs and benefits of international cooperation. Thus, the size of the costs and benefits at both the domestic and the international level will affect a state's decision when to comply.

Governments are likely to comply immediately when the requested corrections to the status quo are minimal. The magnitude of the domestic costs can be a function of several factors. First, the size of the group affects matters. The larger the group affected by a rule change, the more likely a government will delay complying. Size can be measured in several ways. It can include simply the number of people or firms affected by change to the status quo. It can also be measured as the relative importance of a population or industry as a share of the whole economy. For example, if an international agreement calls for the reduction of carbon dioxide emitted by coal-fired power plants, and a country's electricity generation is dominated by these utilities, then we can expect noncompliance to occur.[12]

Yet, size is not everything. Size interacts with the magnitude of costs requested by an international regime or other regime members. The magnitude of the costs can be a function of the "depth of cooperation." If the agreement calls for few changes to the status quo, then even when the agreement affects many, it is unlikely that a government will refuse to comply. Many requests for compliance the European Commission makes are highly technical in nature. Sometimes they only require changes in the wording of a statute or clarification of a rule. At other times the Commission asks the government to make slight changes to existing procedures, but allows the regulation to stay in place to secure it.

The costs of complying can also be a function of the "depth of cooperation." Therefore, for delayed compliance to occur, there must be some material change in the status quo.

Even when a large group is affected or the magnitude of the costs is high, governments may comply, irrespective of the impact compliance has on a powerful interest group. Another factor that affects whether compliance is delayed is whether formal or informal ties exist between the domestic groups bearing the costs of complying and the incumbent government. Some states have open institutions where there is active coordination and consultation between societal and governmental actors. Germany is a well-known example. In contrast, some states develop and implement policies with little consultation of societal actors, such as the exclusion of labor groups in France. Access to lawmakers increases the probability that compliance will be delayed.

Sean Ehrlich calls the points at which interest groups can influence lawmakers "access points" (Ehrlich 2007). In short, these access points include the numbers of representatives in legislative institutions. However, the compliance process does not always require the input of legislators. The Member States have established different processes by which to handle both EU affairs and suspected cases of noncompliance.[13] For example, in France, Belgium and Luxembourg, national parliaments play little role in the compliance process until national legislation is required to change the status quo. In some cases, the societal actors are brought in not only to craft a government's position on EU legislation, but also to decide how best to meet the Commission's legal requirements. How open a bureaucracy is to interest group influence can shape whether the government chooses to comply immediately or not.

Third, a government's decision to comply immediately or wait for a court ruling can depend on whether national political pressure has built around refusal to comply with an international institution's demands. This can come in a variety of forms. For example, national political parties can unite in opposition to compliance. This is often the case in the United States, due to a political or legal culture that is less than enthusiastic about the role of international law in domestic politics and its integration into US law. In the US, political pressure not to comply can spread across all three branches of government. Thus, the likelihood that there is a delay in compliance is also affected by a national legal or political culture's receptivity of international law.

National political pressure can also emerge when an interest group or industry can organize broad-based support among the general population. In some cases the demands the Commission places on a government to change the status quo does not just affect a powerful group or constituency. The required changes can also stimulate opposition among the general population because they affect a widely shared cultural practice or tradition. For example, Chapter 3 discusses a case of noncompliance related to the German beer industry. The Commission demanded less discrimination against beer imports from other EU countries. Although all German consumers would have been better off if there was more competition in the market for beer in Germany, small and medium-sized breweries affected by those imports were able to glean support from the wider German population by framing the problem as one in which a foreign institution was insisting that accepted German tradition was under attack, rather than just their profits.

In summary, whether a Member State chooses to battle a case of noncompliance before the ECJ does not just depend on the size of the group involved and whether the costs are of significant magnitude. It also depends on whether small groups can influence government institutions. Otherwise, governments are likely to comply immediately, as long as the costs for the entire nation are not great. These domestic pressures are then weighed against the international pressures to comply. The international costs include the probability of sanctions, threats of retaliation, the foregoing of larger long-term gains associated with international cooperation, and even the loss of legitimacy in the international system if the case of noncompliance is particularly severe.

In the case of the European Union, compliance almost always occurs once the ECJ has issued a ruling. First, as Zürn and Joerges (2005) show, high levels of legalization secure greater rates of compliance than other mechanisms. In the EU the probability that sanctions will be imposed is small. There are few cases of the Commission helping states to comply after the ECJ has issued its ruling. An ECJ ruling on the matter is sometimes sufficient to cause compliance. First, an ECJ ruling clarifies the law, its meaning and what the accepted solution should be. However, in many cases a government is fully informed about what is required to become compliant. Governments delay until the ECJ issues its decision in order to justify to the affected constituency that change is required. Because the ECJ has legitimacy as the final arbiter, governments almost always comply.

Yet, an ECJ ruling is not the only time when governments choose to comply. In some situations governments will choose not to delay complying because they are also negotiating additional steps of European integration. Noncompliance with an agreement can threaten the credibility of the government during negotiations. The gains that can be made through more international cooperation can exceed domestic pressure. As mentioned earlier, leaders have mixed motives when negotiating agreements. They have domestic groups in favor of cooperation. They also have a constituency of the entire country. Their motives are at least mixed. Thus, when noncompliance threatens the possibility of securing future gains for the entire country, the government is most likely to comply, even before an international court issues its ruling.

The case studies show that a high level of legalization was sufficient to generate compliance. The probability of sanctions or financial assistance did not lead leaders to change state behavior. But can a country be blamed for noncompliance if it does not know what the rules are? If there is so much uncertainty, low levels of precision or high levels of flexibility, concerning the purpose or meaning of an international legal obligation, how can we predict who will violate the law before it happens? If ambiguity in the legal text means that an international court must issue a ruling or consensus over the meaning of the rule, how can noncompliant behavior be identified? Finally, if the meaning of the law is relatively vague or imprecise, it can still be entirely appropriate for the government to defend the status quo. The behavior that either an international institution or other regime members suspect a government of committing may not constitute a violation of the law once a final judgment is rendered or international consensus among regime members is reached. In brief, the suspected violation may not even constitute an infringement of EU law. Law is a fluid institution and evolves (or devolves) over time. Therefore, predicting who and when will violate an international regime is a challenging task.

The precise state activity that domestic or international actors will suspect of being noncompliant cannot always be determined in advance. International organization itself for violating the agreement cannot always be predetermined with precision. Nevertheless, the winners and losers that an international agreement produces can be identified in several ways. First, most obviously, one can turn to the historical record and identify domestic groups (or states) that actively opposed an agreement but lost out.[14] Second, one can examine the reservations national leaders had when bargaining over an agreement and determine whether the costs they were willing to tolerate developed into subsequent violations of that agreement. Another method would be to determine the government's ideal point concerning the agreement and assess the distance between it and the point along the policy spectrum at which the state approved the agreement.[15] Once these costs are estimated, we can assess whether these costs are associated with the problems of noncompliance observed later. Finally, the losers can be identified by examining the general purpose of the agreement, usually what is stated in the treaty or other legal document, and then apply existing social science theories to evaluate whether they explain the general pattern of violations observed.

In the case of the European Union, a key feature of European integration was the establishment of a single internal market that allowed for the free movement of goods and services, capital and people. The key goal was to remove various restrictions on the free movement of goods, services, capital and people and bring down the barriers to intra-European trade among the Member States in order to realize the economic and political goals of a common market and, eventually, economic and monetary union. Some argue the purpose behind integration was the "rescue of the national state" (Urwin 2000) in light of the immense challenges the European countries faced competing in an international system dominated by the United States. Others argue the construction of the single market strengthened various domestic coalitions (Moravcsik 1998). The "founding fathers" of the European Union dreamed of a united Europe that would prevent the great carnage of the two World Wars that claimed millions of lives in the first half of the twentieth century (see Burgess 2000). Economic integration would prevent the discriminatory and retaliatory trade practices of the interwar period that exacerbated the Great Depression. German economic and political power would be encased within a European institutional framework, preventing it from threatening world peace again. While each version of EU history has its strengths and weaknesses, the central component for realizing the vision of a united Europe was the construction of a single market that would liberalize trade within the EU. As a result, the increased economic integration would produce winners and losers.

Alternative outcomes

Noncompliance with an agreement is not the only possible state reaction to changes in the clarity or flexibility of the law, or exogenous shocks that change a state's calculus. Governments can either change the law such that it conforms to their interests or defect from the regime altogether. Garrett and Tsebelis (1996) argue this is the case when considering European legal integration. After the ECJ and the Commission took steps to increase their power by making decisions adverse to the Member States' interests, both bodies backed down (Garrett 1995). Thus, states could redraft agreements or curtail the power of independent international institutions to ensure that an international regime did not impose obligations on states that would be costly. A state could also simply defect from the regime altogether.

Both of these options, however, are likely to be uncommon. First, constant revision of an international rule to redefine compliant or noncompliant behavior is a costly affair. The time and effort of renegotiating a treaty are not always lower than the losses that a state will suffer from having to change the national status quo. In the complicated world of decision making in the EU, adopting a new EU regulation that trumps the Commission's demands for compliance by changing the rule itself is highly unlikely. Second, renegotiation of a treaty or specific regulation is most likely to occur only when a large member or group of members are substantially affected by the unintended requirements of international law. Whatever the new costs that a change in the law or agreement is generating, they are highly likely to be asymmetrical in nature. Therefore, unless the new legal requirement represents some type of radical change, affects enough members equally, or a few large states substantially, it is unlikely that a significant number of regime members will cooperate effectively to renegotiate the law. Renegotiation of a treaty also carries the risk for regime members that the original purpose for cooperation is abandoned, or additional tasks are included in the bargaining process that the government hopes to exclude. Thus, unless the costs of compliance are severe, it is unlikely that states will react to cases of noncompliance by renegotiating an agreement such that, simply by redefining compliance, they are no longer noncompliant.

Retaliation is also a possible response. Under Article 259 of the EC Treaty, a Member State can report possible legal infringements to the Commission. Yet, records on the application of EU law, compiled by the Commission, show that notifications by Member States that others are violating the law are relatively rare. One of the chief reasons is that every Member State not only has the incentive to cheat on the agreement, it could also face additional retaliation from other

Member States. It is also difficult for another Member State to detect noncompliance. Retaliation is also most likely to be effective when the threat of punishment or exclusion of a state from future benefits is most credible. Yet, even in the EU, where no state could even formally withdraw from the EU until recently, Member State governments refrain from reporting the suspected cases of noncompliance in other Member States.[16]

Complete defection from the regime is one final possible action if noncompliance occurs. Noncompliance is not a serious issue if states act in their own interest to defy their international legal obligations or leave a regime altogether when complying is contrary to their national interests. But complete defection from a regime is also unlikely to be a normal occurrence in the international system. Again, states need to perform a cost–benefit analysis before choosing to defect. If they do, they forgo all the gains of future cooperation. As long as the time horizon of cooperation is sufficiently long, governments are likely to trade-off the small, short-term costs of complying for the long-term gains of future cooperation. And if a government does want to cooperate in the future, its reputation will be sullied if it chooses to defect. Second, other states are not likely to act neutrally to another member's defection. They can also retaliate against a state for defecting. Finally, institutional regimes are sometimes delegated the powers of enforcement to prevent noncompliance or push states into compliance if it occurs (Guzman 2002, 2008). While the effectiveness of different enforcement strategies can be questioned, and deserves more scholarly attention, the claim that states defect from international agreements or institutions whenever the latter are not in a state's interests is unrealistic.

A final possible outcome is, of course, that the European Court of Justice agrees with the Member State that the suspected legal infringement does not violate EU law. There are at least two reasons why this occurs. First, the Member State government makes a rational argument that the status quo is compliant and the Court finds it persuasive (Kratochwil 1989, Panke 2007). Second, the Court fears retaliation from the Member States themselves and rules in favor of the government. Several scholars suggest that the ECJ does not rule against Member States when they know the costs of compliance are prohibitive (Garrett 1995, Carrubba *et al.* 2008). For reasons explained above, these conditions are unlikely. Instead, it is more likely the Member State government has effectively persuaded the judicial tribunal that the suspected infringement does not constitute noncompliance.

Selection bias, scope and methods

Studying the politics of compliance with international law is an exercise fraught with methodological issues. The difficulties are several. They include various forms of selection bias. This section deals with each in turn and then outlines the contents of the following chapters of this book.

The first issue to arise when studying compliance in international affairs is selection bias. As the number of explanations for why states almost always comply with international law proliferated, Downs *et al.* (1996) gave the study of compliance some pause by arguing that the reasons why states comply so often is because they are complying with agreements that require little change in the status quo and they would change the status quo in any case. Because of domestic constraints shaping state bargaining positions, states make agreements with which they know they will have little trouble complying (Downs and Rocke 1995). States select themselves into an international commitment and, thus, all the good news about compliant behavior is nothing surprising.

Does selection bias in this respect affect this study of the *cross-national* variation in *noncompliance* within the *same* legal regime? There are good reasons to suggest that it does not. First, the motives states have in joining international institutions, such as the European Union, are highly mixed and complex.[17] For example, France was partially interested in committing to the EC Treaty in the hope of integrating a resurgent and rearmed Germany into a network of institutional ties that would constrain its future actions. It was also interested in having a larger market for its consumer goods and a larger safety net for its farmers in the form of the Common Agricultural Policy (Moravcsik 1998). In turn, the German government was interested in European integration for the same foreign policy reasons as the French, but also foresaw the advantages of a single market for its industrial and manufacturing exports. Yet the EC Treaty that these two countries signed went far beyond these issues in scope. It included articles related not just to the customs union and CAP, but also to the free movement of capital and people and the establishment of a European Parliament. Although integration along these lines took some time, there are numerous issues that the EC Treaty covered that cannot be easily attributed directly back to the domestic interests or constraints that a national government was considering when committing to an international agreement. In a wide-ranging and expansive document such as the EC Treaty and subsequent agreements, it is difficult to argue that national governments rationally choose to bargain over every single element of an agreement and that those positions are based on pre-existing domestic constraints or national interests and thus ensure that the agreement is sufficiently shallow.

Moreover, especially in the case of the EU, the scope and character of the agreement changes over time, which national governments cannot always anticipate. As the EU expanded in terms of the number of Member States and policies covered and also deepened in terms of governing capacity, the Member States still eventually chose to comply with these changes, even though they had little role in shaping these outcomes and it would often not be in their general interest to do so. For example, when the United Kingdom joined the then-EC in 1973, the government could not have anticipated that several years later domestic interest groups would use EU law to change social and gender policy in the UK (Alter and Vargas 2000). All demonstrate how difficult it is for a national government to anticipate how institutional membership will affect its national interests over time.[18] Of course, the European Union may be a unique institution in terms how much it now governs and shapes national policies (Hooghe and

Marks, 2001). However, the ability of international institutions to expand in policy scope and mission is not unique to the EU. These institutions have a "pathology" of their own. As their bureaucratic cultures develop, they expand their scope of authority, and spread new norms of appropriate behavior (Barnett and Finnemore 1999). Thus, the reasons states *eventually* comply can be independent from those related to when they made their initial international commitments.

Second, in contrast to some previous studies of compliance with international law, this study of Member State behavior in the EU focuses on *noncompliance* and its variety of forms. My goal here is not to explain why states comply with law beyond the nation state or compare international regimes in terms of which one secures more member compliance than another. Instead, this book accounts for noncompliance with an international institution's rules, why it varies across its members, and when in the compliance process states will choose to comply. Therefore, assuming that there is a compliance gap, this book aims only to understand why it affects members of the same regime differently. Third and finally, even if domestic interests do constrain or shape the entire content of an agreement, there are always winners and losers produced by the international bargaining process. Therefore, while domestic incentives or national benefits may explain why the Member States have committed to cooperate, the other side of the political ledger, the domestic costs or national harms, can also explain why the Member States subsequently violate their commitments.

The second methodological issue related to selection bias is whether states are complying with an international agreement because of the agreement or international institution itself or with regard to conditions prior to their commitment (von Stein 2005). When assessing whether international agreements generate greater compliance success by comparing only states that signed on to an agreement with those that did not, it is difficult to assess whether compliance by the signatories was due to belonging to the regime or because of the conditions that motivated them to sign on. Since this study concerns itself with explaining noncompliance, rather than compliance, and assessing the independent effects international institutions have on state behavior, this type of selection bias is not an issue. In fact, this study shows that the environmental conditions that governments confront *change* over time, and thus noncompliance will occur frequently while states are a member of an international regime. But, at least in the case of the European Union, this does not lead a Member State to exit from the regime or permanently sustain a violation in all cases. If it were true, this would lead us to conclude that the regime or institution has failed and is unable to affect state behavior. In contrast, we should acknowledge that violations of international law occur all the time and states are often discovered not to be fulfilling their international legal commitments. But it is rash to conclude from that fact that the international organization is failing to generate compliance with international law. Instead, compliance with international law should be considered a process that includes several stages and types of outcomes. The likelihood that states will comply depends on whether the costs of complying are concentrated, but of a small magnitude, or large but diffuse. In short, although selection bias issues related to determining the independent effect regimes have in securing compliance will not affect this study's findings, we should be more careful in dismissing the effect of international institutions just because we observe some noncompliance taking place in the short or medium term after regime members sign on. If not, what we are observing is only one stage in the compliance process.

There is one alternative form of selection bias that can affect the results presented. This form of selection bias is related both to why violations occur and to their varying distribution across states and time. First, the Commission strategizes in terms of which cases to pursue. If the Commission, and sometimes the ECJ, is concerned about maximizing its authority while preventing backlash by the Member States (Garrett 1995), it may select minor cases from less influential states to prosecute. Alternatively, the legal doctrine and authority the Commission is seeking to develop directs it to prosecute some types of legal violations more than others, and these types of regulatory practice suspected of being violations may be disproportionately taking place in one or more countries more often than in others. The focus of the Commission's attention on a particular state or regulatory rule can also change over time, changing the cross-national distribution of violations over time. Finally, the distribution of infringements over time can also decrease or increase because of the Commission's changing legal interpretations of the EC Treaty. Thus, the domestic regulation in Greece in 1985 is no longer considered to be noncompliant in Italy in 1992. Again, this is a function of the flexibility and precision of international law.

These issues of selection bias are serious and directly affect the ability to conclude that the reasons for noncompliance are independent of the Commission's legal strategy or political goals and exist because of the adjustment costs firms face. The reasons why we can discount this factor are discussed in Chapter 3. In summary, there is little evidence to support any of these claims. First, the Commission chooses cases to prosecute on the sole basis of the evidence available, a legal interpretation of whether the regulation conforms to the EC Treaty or not, and then moves ahead in the compliance process on the basis of the response by the Member State. Second, targeting specific countries for prosecution or not is highly discouraged and monitored in Brussels. Finally, the regulatory issues that the Commission decides to address may vary over time, but they are unlikely to shift the distribution of infringements across the Member States significantly over time.

Related to the issue of selection bias generated by strategic behavior by the Commission is the question whether the cases of noncompliance themselves are independent of any political or economic pattern. Instead, the regulatory barriers the Commission chooses to prosecute are based solely on a set of legal criteria and interpretations. During interviews, Commission officials repeatedly asserted that the only motivations shaping their decisions to initiate Article 258 proceedings were whether one can reasonably conclude, on the basis of legal rationale and the justifications of the Member State government for the trade barrier, that a strong legal case can be made that the suspected piece of legislation constitutes a violation of the EC Treaty.

While the expertise and independence of Commission officials responsible for enforcing the EC Treaty and other forms of EU law should not be doubted, they are not always aware of the patterns of prosecution that develop as a result of applying their legal rationales. Although they are applying EU law seemingly independent of politics, this does not mean the resulting pattern of states prosecuted will be entirely random. The distribution of violations across states, with Denmark committing some of the fewest while Greece and Italy commit the most, shows that some violations are repeatedly occurring in some states and not others. If the distribution of infringements of EU law recur across policy areas where different legal principles are involved, across time, as the law is changing and transforming itself, then it is safe to conclude that the reasons some Member States are violating EU law more than others are independent from the legal doctrine and regulations the Commission is attempting to enforce. Just as bank robbers rob banks because that is where they money is, the Commission is prosecuting some states more often than others for violating EU law because that is where the greatest amount of noncompliance is.

Scope

In order to observe the types of noncompliant behavior this book discusses, the regime to which states belong must be somewhat formally or informally legalized. The legalization school, summarized best by Michael Zürn (2005), argues that compliance is best secured when there is a high level of juridification and internalization (Zürn and Joerges 2005). Internalization of international law happens when "norms above and beyond national societies only attain full legal status when they are legally, socially and politically internalized by those to whom they are addressed" (Koh 1997, Raustilia 1995). According to Zürn (2005), internalization contains two dimensions – civil and legal. While legal internalization refers to the fact that international norms directly affect their addressees and do not require national legal implementation to have effect, civil internationalization refers to the quality by which individuals are allocated specific rights that are actionable and these individuals can seek redress directly in national or international courts (Zürn 2005).

Legal juridification refers to "the process by which it is ensured that regulations fulfill certain criteria, such as clarity, pertinence, stringency, adaptability and a high degree of consistency, both within themselves and in relation to other laws" (Zürn 2005: 23). This process, in turn, contains three elements, according to the legalization approach of Abbott (2000) and Abbott *et al.* (2001). The rule or regulatory process should have a sense of "obligation," a high level of "precision," and clear "delegation," whereby a third party has the authority to implement, interpret and apply the rules as well as settle disputes over time (Zürn 2005). High levels of internalization do enhance compliance with law beyond the nation state, as is shown in the case study comparisons of legal regimes at different levels of governance in Zürn and Joerges (2005).

It is this last component of juridification that is important to my model of noncompliance. Delayed compliance cannot, by definition, occur without some level of delegation. Delegation implies two central components. First, the parties to the legal dispute belong to some regime or international arbiter that has jurisdiction not only over the parties, but also over the substance of the infringement. Either the international arbiter or other regime members have some authority over the matter to make a conclusive judgment. Second, the definitive ruling and whoever's authority to settle the dispute are perceived as legitimate. The level of delegation or to whom legal disputes are delegated can vary. For example, many legal disputes are settled by international, independent regulatory agencies, particularly in the areas of high policy complexity such as health issues, intellectual property rights, or violations of international codes of conduct by athletes, whereby the addressees are mainly individuals. The International Monetary Fund assesses whether its members are meeting their obligations regarding the removal of capital restrictions and opening their current account (Simmons 2000). In the most highly juridified regimes, international courts, such as the International Criminal Court, the European Court for Human Rights or the World Trade Organization's dispute settlement tribunal, can issue rulings whereby the parties can be both public and private actors and must be obeyed.

This is complicated by the fact that all monitoring institutions or other members have incentives not to prosecute the offenders. The independent authority need not be a court, however. It could also be the international community as a whole. This does not imply, however, that noncompliance is not taking place before a court or other body issues a ruling. The goals and policies that states agree to when concluding treaties or joining an international regime always contain some general principles or rules that the parties plan to abide by. One can then objectively assess whether the parties have abided by their commitment *ex post*. Certainly, the specific practices must be adjudicated before they can actually constitute noncompliance. In the case of the German beer law, the German government may believe and vociferously argue that the Beer Purity Law did not constitute a violation of Article 34 ECT. It argued that the law was a legitimate method of protecting a German consumer's health. From a legal perspective, then, the Beer Law did not constitute a violation of EU law until the ECJ ruled that it did. In short, a person or country is presumed innocent until proven guilty.

Yet this standard is too high for the purposes of assessing noncompliance comparatively over time or across the members of an international regime. First, facts always exist "on the ground" such that the independent researcher can make a relatively rigorous or credible assessment whether a specific behavior by an individual or state is a violation of an international rule or norm. Second, placing violations in comparative perspective, as social scientists, helps us account for the possible causes of their repeated behavior. Situations will develop whereby some social or political practice is deemed completely legal before an independent ruling and then perceived illegal afterwards. For example, legally based racial segregation in American public schools was deemed constitutional until *Plessey v. Ferguson* was overturned by a later US Supreme Court decision in 1954 in *Brown v. Board of Education* and, thus, segregation is now deemed unconstitutional. But we can stipulate that segregation violated the human rights of African-Americans before and after the Supreme Court's decision. The fact that some state practices were legal before 1954 and illegal after, shows how instances of noncompliance are not independent of changes in the legal environment. In short, the distribution of legal violations over time and countries can be dependent on how the law itself evolves. However, because of *stare decisis*, in which legal precedent is given strong deference by judges and courts, at least in customary legal systems, international and EU law is stable enough such that suspected violations of the law can be reasonably discovered and explained before an independent authority issues a final ruling in a specific case. In short, my argument treats states as guilty until proven innocent.

Finally, even a casual reader will notice that the units of analysis here are national governments or states. The addressees of these international rules and legal obligations discussed are always states. Individuals or groups within states also have legal obligations under international law, whether customary or treaty-based. EU law, which is supranational, imposed legal obligations on private as well as public actors. In addition, private individuals have standing under EU law to bring cases of noncompliance against their own governments, other national governments, and other private parties, through national or EU courts. Yet, while an important feature of EU law, an individual as the addressee of international law is not a common feature of other regional or international regimes. In addition, the world of public international law is legally more developed than that of private international law. Treaties, international accords, protocols and other forms of international law are more ubiquitous in the international system than regimes that bind private individuals. In order to develop a theoretical framework that can easily travel across international regimes, I choose to focus on states as the sole actors under international law.

In conclusion, there is still a strong case to be made that states do not construct agreements that are not in their self-interest (Goldsmith and Posner 2005). If true, then we are least likely to expect noncompliance to occur in the EU and in countries that would most benefit from integration. Thus, these forms of international law constitute a "hard case" for my theoretical model. In an international regime as legally as robust as the EU, we should expect those countries whose interests are most served by European integration to comply most often. In addition, over time, as the law becomes more precise, we should expect more noncompliance until states either remove themselves from the regime or refrain from committing legal violations.

Methods

To test this theory of noncompliance behavior, this book uses historical process tracing of four cases of EU legal infringements to demonstrate this model at work. In Chapters 3 and 4, two country-case comparisons are brought forward that trace the origins and process of compliance. The theory of noncompliance presented here has, essentially, three parts. First, noncompliance arises when the "losers" produced by an international treaty were not compensated during its negotiation. Next, exogenous shocks to the economy that were not anticipated by national leaders at the time of negotiation, coupled with the demands of the international agreement, can cause noncompliance to occur. Third, the legal case studies show how small groups bear the brunt of the costs of compliance, while the gains of cooperation are diffused across national societies. Because of the political pressures these groups bring to bear on national governments, or in tandem with the default position of a government not to comply, national governments defend the national regulation that gives an unfair trade advantage to domestic industry. The legal arguments governments use to defend the status quo are rarely successful, and often hardly credible, as the decisions of both the ECJ and the Commission attest.

Through paired comparison in two areas related to the single European market, we can observe the mechanisms of noncompliance at work. First, two cases of noncompliance related to the free movement of goods are discussed, specifically alcoholic beverages in Germany and videocassettes in France. Second, two cases in the area of state aid, or unlawful government subsidies, are explored in relation to regional banks in Germany and the automobile industry in the UK. These countries were selected because they lie at different ends of the noncompliance spectrum. France commits many violations related to the single market, Germany is roughly in the middle, while the United Kingdom commits comparatively fewer. They also possess three different legal traditions and have varying levels of interest in economic integration and the power of EU supranational institutions. In order to control for these factors, qualitative methods are appropriate. Second, if the same reasons for noncompliance and escalation through the compliance are present in all three countries, then we can be confident that the causes of noncompliance and the type of compliance behavior observed as a consequence are characteristic of many other violations across the remaining EU Member States.

In the country case studies, historical evidence provided by secondary sources is used to determine which actors most likely lost as a result of the agreements the major Member States adopted. In addition, the long-term gains compared to the short-term losses for each country are discussed. Then I show how exogenous shocks to each country's economy exacerbated some of the costs of complying with the EC Treaty's demands. Finally, through process tracing of each legal infringement from the point at which the legal case originated to its termination, I show how some firms put significant pressure on governments to delay compliance. In each of these cases, however, governments were not willing to sacrifice the long-term gains associated with European economic integration in order to protect a particular domestic industry. In one case, the French films case, the government was actually victorious in its dispute with the other firms seeking less protection. However, through qualitative analysis, we can see that it was not for the reasons often cited in the scholarly literature on European legal integration. Instead of ruling in favor of the French government because of fears of retaliation, for which there is little empirical evidence, the Court found France's regulatory practice legitimate in this case. Yet the reason for noncompliance in the French films case is comparable to violations that occur in other countries. As a result, we can also be confident that the reasons for noncompliance with the EC Treaty are not particular to each individual case, inasmuch as every suspected legal infringement has its own unique circumstance and context in which it emerges.

Plan of the rest of the book

The remaining chapters of this book explain the origins of noncompliance in the European Union. Although the EU is a highly legalized regime and, as Zürn and Joerges (2005) show, secures compliance better than both international and national regimes, noncompliance still occurs frequently. Not only does it vary across countries and time; some countries delay until the ECJ issues a ruling more often than others. This shows that the attributes of a highly legalized international regime are having a differential effect among its members.

The case studies that follow explore different patterns of compliance behavior in three countries. In Chapter 3, two cases of noncompliance in two countries strongly supportive of European integration are explored. In spite of being the largest and most powerful countries in the EU, they both decided to comply eventually, but only after there was a Court ruling. Neither country succeeded in securing payoffs for the losers generated by the EC Treaty. Furthermore, even though France won its case before the Court of Justice and Germany lost, the dynamics associated with noncompliance were similar in both countries. In Chapter 4, two case studies in the area of state-aid policy, a highly legalized area of EU law, are compared in Germany and the United Kingdom. In both the Rover and the Landesbanken cases, key national benefits were at stake. However, because national support failed to develop and specific long-term interests were at stake during the compliance process, the governments of both countries complied before the Court issued its rulings. As a result, these case studies both exhibit variation on the dependent variable and use both most-similar and most-different case study designs to explains similar patterns of noncompliant behavior.

In the conclusion, Chapter 5, I summarize the book's argument and central findings. Then I briefly discuss the Maastricht criteria and the rules concerning the establishment of the single European currency, where we observe complete noncompliance for two reasons. First, the euro's legal regime did not reach sufficient levels of legalization and national governments were not willing to sacrifice short-term losses for the long-term gains of maintaining compliance. Finally, I illustrate how the difficulties governments have dealing with the pressures coming from two levels shape the debate over the legitimacy of international law.

3 Noncompliance and national tradition

Enforcing the free movement of goods in Germany and France

The single internal market represents one of the crowning achievements of European integration. Following the creation of the European Coal and Steel Community in 1956, the Member States pursued a conscious strategy of increased economic interdependence to avoid the misery and tragedy of nationalist conflict that characterized the first half of the twentieth century. The centerpiece of that economic strategy was the integration of national markets. Firms would be able to sell their wares across the EU without discrimination. A EU citizen would be free to work and reside in any Member State he or she wished. National borders would no longer stand in the way of the free flow of capital. Yet, accomplishing that task was more challenging politically than perhaps the founders of the European Union envisioned.

The obstacles that arose to European economic integration were deep and widespread. Despite the commitment by many Member States to a liberal economic order within the confines of European borders, downturns in the international economy, powerful interest groups, or simple bureaucratic inertia prevented the full realization of the single -market concept. Many of the cases of noncompliance that emerged resulted from a small sector of firms bearing the costs of fulfilling the larger goals of completing the single market. Not only were these costs concentrated, but they were also of a high magnitude for these groups. In the case of the Beer Purity Law, or *Reinheitsgebot*, the Commission set about lifting a nontariff barrier that provided significant amounts of protection to a declining industry in Germany. Interest groups representing the small and medium-sized brewers in Bavaria lobbied their representatives and urged them not to comply with the Commission's legal demands. They also generated widespread support for their causes. By appealing to national traditions, the brewing industry hoped to create significant electoral pressure on politicians to refrain from changing the status quo. The brewers' association also used special access to powerful lawmakers to influence the government's decision to litigate the case before the ECJ. Pressure not to comply continued even after the ECJ issued a ruling averse for their interests. The German government attempted to maintain legal protections for the German brewing industry for several years after the ECJ's ruling, risking economic punishment by the Commission.

Despite the high domestic political costs of complying, the German government did eventually decide to remove all forms of protection the Commission deemed discriminatory. Germany was not willing to sacrifice the long-term gains of cooperation and the creation of the single market. Germany has served as one of the strongest supporters of European integration. For both foreign policy and economic reasons, Germany, together with France, stands as one of the key motors of European integration. Since the early years of the European Union, the German government's position has been to encase its growing economic and political power within European institutions. At the same time Germany, as the largest exporter to the rest of Europe, saw great economic advantages in pursuing economic integration. Yet, Germany could not ensure that there would not be unintended consequences as a result. Because of exogenous changes to the European market for beer and the Commission's decision to enforce the doctrine of mutual recognition, another unintended consequence of legal integration, the German government faced a difficult political dilemma. It could either satisfy the interests of a few or continue to accrue the long-term gains of future cooperation. They chose the latter, but revisions to the Beer Purity Law set the stage for growing opposition and skepticism about the European project among Germans.

In France, numerous governments always faced a challenge of balancing the costs and benefits of European integration. On the positive side of the ledger, France strongly supported European integration to contain German power and use its political influence to shape EU policies in its favor. On the other side of the ledger, France was both skeptical of the growing supranational authority of the EU and wary of adjusting to the EU's increasing demands for economic liberalization. Throughout the history of France's EU membership, the government was repeatedly forced to weigh the long-term, diffuse benefits brought by European economic integration against the concentrated and high costs of continued reforms of the French economy.

As the *Cinéthèque SA* case shows, France faced a significant and wholly unanticipated threat to its film industry as it pursued its interests at the EU level. As in the German case, the French film industry faced growing European and, more importantly, global economic pressure. The French attempted to protect their industry through content regulations, mainly in the form of how films could be watched. And, in this case, the French government achieved victory at the EU level. The ruling in *Cinéthèque* also set the stage for changes to EU case law itself. Through the famous *Keck* decision, the ECJ would reverse itself and limit the challenges traders could raise against national regulations deemed discriminatory to EU imports. As a result, *Cinéthèque* shows not only that Member States do not always lose when they go before the ECJ. They also bring about changes to international law such that it is more in line with their interests. Therefore, not all cases of noncompliance lead to required changes in the status quo. When considering the politics of noncompliance, this is an outcome that is always a possibility. Whether it is the result of a regime member flexing its power or an international institution reconsidering the costs and benefits of enforcing the EC

Treaty, cases of noncompliance can lead to changes in the international rule itself to bring noncompliance behavior into compliance.

This chapter begins by outlining the development of the single market, the dominant national interests of France and Germany at the time and then identifies who the losers from the Treaty of Rome were likely to be in each country. The next section outlines the development of the doctrine of the free movement of goods and how it relates to national regulatory practices. As the Commission and ECJ worked together to enforce the EC Treaty, they developed the doctrine of mutual recognition. The doctrine of "majoritarian activism" was intended to serve as a compromise between deregulation across the EU and allowing states to retain qualitative barriers to the free movement of goods. In spite of this "compromise," the Commission still targeted specific national regulations that discriminated against imports from other Member States that, in effect, protected uncompetitive industries. The third section then traces the compliance process in two controversial areas: the Beer Purity Law in Germany and protections for French cinemas in France. I show how cases of noncompliance developed, how their costs were concentrated and of a high magnitude, which led their governments to litigate these cases before the European Court of Justice. Although Germany lost its case before the ECJ, and France was victorious, they both demonstrate the key argument of this book: the origins of noncompliance result from the unanticipated costs of regime membership, their high concentration and magnitude, and how those affected can mobilize national support through appeal to national sentiments and through access to important political supporters.

Detecting the losers: interests and disinterests in European integration in Germany and France

Together, France and Germany serve as the engines for European integration.[1] When the motor was running, European integration progressed. When it stalled, integration slowed along with it. The Treaty of Rome, the basis for the Treaty of the European Communities, was primarily the product of their historical cooperation. During multiple bargaining stages, these two countries shared enough interests in common to purse the integration of their economies. Through lowest-common-denominator bargaining, these two governments sought to maximize the gains of European cooperation and institution building, while minimizing the costs. If the agreements they concluded were "shallow," in that the Treaty of Rome primarily reflected their interests, then the agreements would require few changes to the status quo. We would expect, therefore, these countries to commit few violations of EU law. If they led the process of European integration and secured their interests over the preferences of others, especially the smaller states, then they should comply more often than others. Finally, according to the management school, as Germany and France are two of the wealthiest countries in the EU, with highly effective bureaucracies and sufficient resources, we would expect noncompliance to occur seldom. The empirical evidence supports none of these hypotheses. Instead, France violates the EC Treaty more often than most

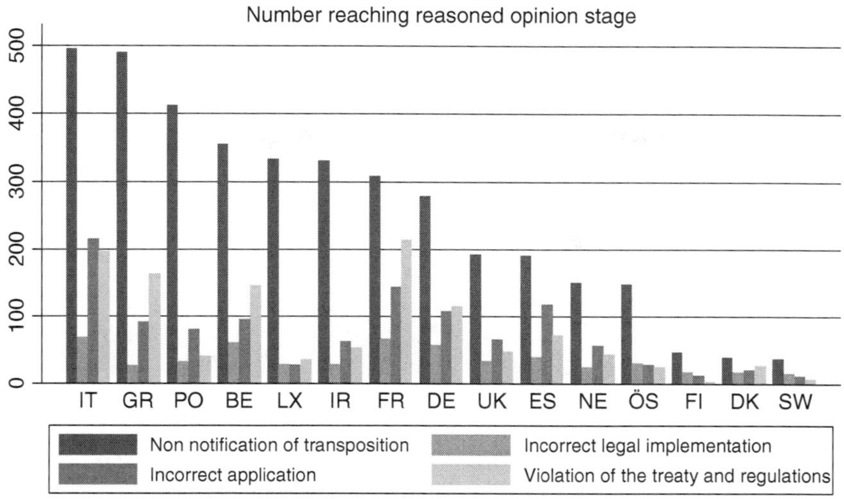

Figure 3.1 Total number of violations by type of EU law.

Source: Annual Reports on the Montioring the Application of EU Law 1978–2002 [European Commission]

other Member States. Despite Germany's strong political and economic interests in completing the single market and European integration in general, it also commits many violations of EU law and falls somewhere in the middle of the cross-national distribution (see Figure 3.1).

Problems of noncompliance emerged for both of these countries, for several reasons. Bargaining at the EU level would always produce domestic costs for important constituents. Even when governments seek to obtain the best possible agreements, they cannot obtain all the side-payments and other forms of compensation to prevent some domestic groups from experiencing net losses as a result of the agreement. These sacrifices are made both to secure larger economic gains for the rest of the country and to create a foundation for future cooperation.

German losers

Among the EU's founding members, no country was as supportive of the EC and its goals than the Federal Republic. As one of its strongest supporters, it was willing to sacrifice several key domestic constituencies on the altar of European integration. As a result, there would be winners and losers. To some extent, Germany's interests in European integration depend on which theoretical approach is employed to explain integration itself. Whether a rational institutionalist or a social constructivist approach is employed to explain German foreign policy *vis-à-vis* the EU, they should not be viewed necessarily as competing with each other. In some circumstances, they are actually complementary. They both produce valid arguments for why Germany agreed to increased European economic integration. The economic and political sacrifices and possible costs associated with complying with the EC Treaty can be detected during and after the bargaining over the Treaty. We can also see that the German government did not fully anticipate the consequences of the agreement, namely the development of the doctrine of mutual recognition and its impact on domestic industrial sectors.

According to the enforcement school of noncompliance, Germany's record of non-compliance with the EC Treaty depends on the degree to which its interests are satisfied by policies that the EU pursues. Andrew Moravcsik (1998) provides a good overview of Germany's national interests at various moments during the integration process. In short, from the rationalist perspective, Germany's prime motivation for integration was to expand the markets for its exports. And Germany did experience significant gains as a result (see Figure 3.2). While these gains are large, they are diffused across the German population.

During negotiations over the Treaty of Rome, both Germany and France sought to obtain the long-term gains of European integration. They did try to minimize the costs of economic integration. For Germany, the central goals of integration were to open larger markets for its export-based economy (Moravcsik 1998). The customs union would be completed on a fixed schedule. Quotas would be eliminated according to a negotiated and specific formula. But, interestingly, one of the key elements of the Treaty, now Articles 34 through 37, which banned quantitative and qualitative barriers to trade that have an equivalent effect, was inserted by a mid-level customs official (Moravcsik 1998: 146, citing Küsters 1982).

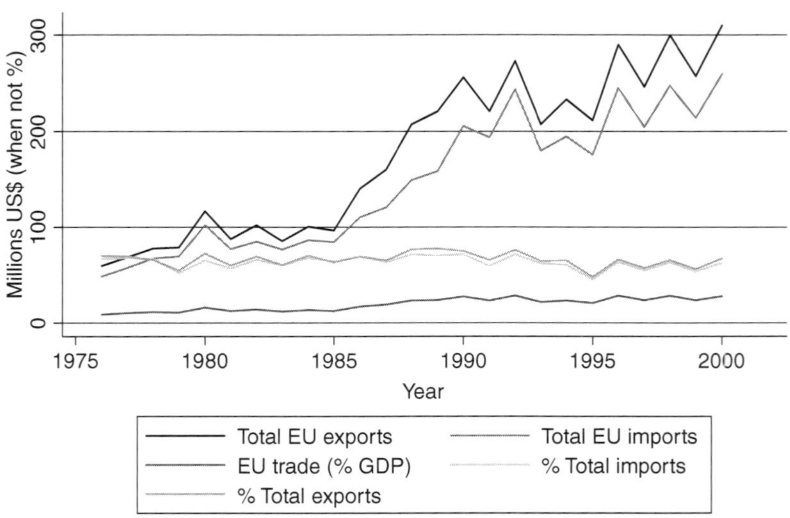

Figure 3.2 German trade with the EU over time.

Source: OECD

The minor attention this clause was given supports the hypothesis that governments are not aware of all of the possible implications of the agreement they sign. In addition, not all of the possible losers disadvantaged by signing up to the EC Treaty were adequately compensated. Germany's export sector, led by the *Bundesverband der deutschen Industrie*, strongly supported the Treaty. In contrast, the nontradables sector, which depended on protectionist regulations, would resist the growing legal demands that Germany should comply with EU law.

The reasons for French support of European integration mirror those of Germany's. The growing exports sector in France, led by the *Conseil National du Patronat Français* (CNPF), pushed for integration in order to expand markets for its automobile, electronic engineering and financial firms (Moravcsik 1998: 108). Most importantly, France's greatest source of comparative advantage, its agricultural sector, would have new outlets for export of its perennial surpluses. For Germany, European integration was another step towards its rehabilitation in order to re-enter the international scene. French officials believed the European Union was a venue in which it could effectively exert its influence and project its power, while also combating American hegemony on the Continent (Balme and Woll 2005).[2]

Yet France could not secure full protection for the possible losers generated by the EC Treaty. First, France accepted the seeds of supranationalism. Although a qualified majority for approving legislation was not initially introduced and was limited to specific policy areas, it became operational once the Treaty went into full effect. In addition, during the drafting of the Treaty, legal experts inserted Article 267, which allowed national courts to send inquiries to the European Court of Justice to obtain preliminary judgments about suspected conflicts between national and EU law. The legal supremacy of EU law then emerged through an alliance between lower-level national courts and the ECJ (Alter 2001, Burley and Mattli 1993). In Rome the French government also conceded that the EU would be fundamentally oriented towards liberalizing national markets, rather than the *dirigiste* economy of France. As a result, many of the firms that benefitted from state protection in France faced the probability that the EU courts would challenge the regulatory protections they enjoyed.

The legal integration of the single market

The creation of EU legal supremacy was not the only unintended consequence of European integration. The content of the law as it related to the free movement of goods was another. One of the primary purposes behind the construction of the single market was the free flow of goods, services, capital, and even people across national boundaries. The original first articles listed in the Treaty of Rome of 1956 related to the free movement of goods.[3] The main focus of European economic integration in the 1950s and 1960s was the removal of all tariffs, quotas, and duties or charges that discriminated against goods among the original six members. Title 1 lays down the legal basis for the establishment of a customs union and, later, the common market. Articles 28 through 33 remove all national tariffs, charges and duties on exports and imports from within the common market and establish a common external tariff.[4] The legal center of the free movement of goods lies, however, with Articles 34 and 37. These articles remove all quantitative and qualitative restrictions on the free movement of goods, respectively, including "all measures having equivalent effect." One of the unintended consequences of legal integration was the slow growth of a legal doctrine that would affect industries that could not effectively compete in Europe if national regulations protecting them from EU imports were lifted. Thus, the legal debate over the meaning of this clause lies at the center of the politics of complying with EU law in the area of the free movement of goods.[5]

Legal jurisprudence in the area of the free movement of goods has been vital in shaping the legal relationship between a Member State and the EU, the proper role of the state and its ability to regulate the market, and, albeit to a lesser extent, the legitimacy of the European Court of Justice itself. In the early days of ECJ jurisprudence, Articles 23–31 of the EC Treaty were the basis from which to develop a distinct supranational legal entity. Several key elements of the EU legal order arose through litigation related to the free movement of goods. For example, the doctrine of *direct effect*, in which Community law is automatically effective and has authority in a Member State's territory, emerged from a dispute over a tariff that Dutch authorities assessed on ureaformaldehyde imported from Germany.[6] The doctrine of EU legal supremacy was established when an Italian citizen sued the national Italian electric company under Article 31 of the Treaty for unlawful monopolistic practices in *Costa v. ENEL*.[7] Additional litigation under Title 1 of the EC Treaty also reasserted supremacy of EU law in *Simmenthal II*.[8] While the ECJ was attempting to find a solution to fundamental conflicts between national and EC law in these cases – for example, whether an Italian court could invalidate a national law when it conflicts with EU law – the initial basis for this and many other disputes that established the EU legal infrastructure arose out of disagreements over the proper exercise of the state's regulatory power regarding its own national markets.

Disputes over the proper role of state regulation constitute a significant plurality of the number of EU legal violations committed by Member States. As Figure 3.3 illustrates, violations of the EC Treaty articles related to the internal market occupy a large share, approximately 38 percent, of the total number of infringements that Member States have committed since 1978.

Violations in the policy areas of employment and social affairs as well as agriculture are also quite numerous, but comprise only one-third of those committed under the internal market (see Table 3.1). There also seems to be a general match between the cross-national distribution of the total number of EC Treaty infringements and the distribution of the total number of infringements related to both the internal market and the free movement of goods (see Figure 3.4).[9] Thus, the single internal market, and the free movement of goods in particular, serve as a promising area of study if we wish to explain why states violate EU law.

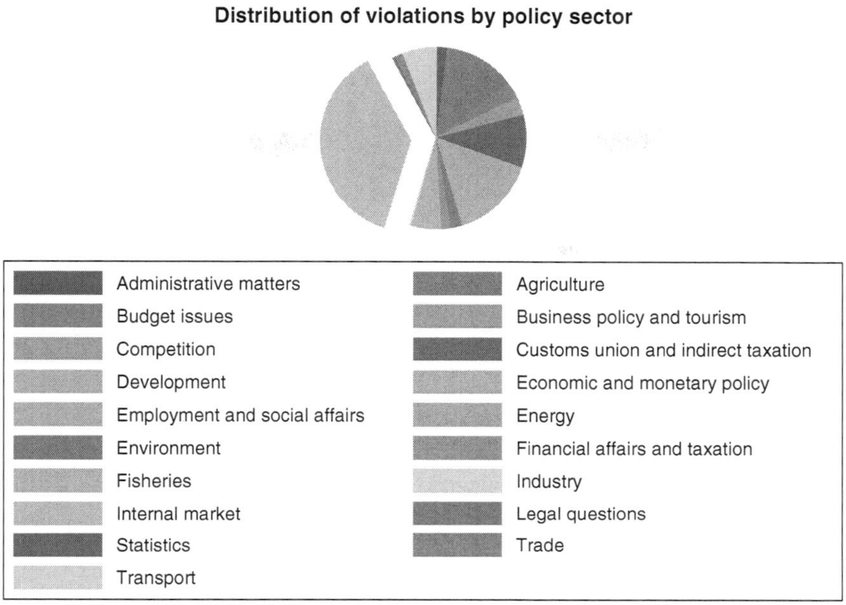

Figure 3.3 Policy distribution of violations.

ECJ jurisprudence in the area of the free movement of goods played the most significant role in defining the purpose of the common market and the proper role of national governmental power *vis-à-vis* the European economy. The changing definitions of what constituted a violation would affect whether Member States complied with EU law or not. The most important elements of the Treaty that relate to the free movement of goods are Articles 34 and 35, which prohibit any restriction on imports and exports, respectively, on the free movement of goods within the Community, including "measures having equivalent effect." Yet, Article 36 states that the Member States could still justify any obstacle to the free movement of goods on the grounds "of public morality, public policy or public security; the protection of health and life of humans, animals or plants; the protection of national treasures possessing artistic, historic or archaeological value; or the protection of industrial and commercial property."[10] In the absence of significant European legislation to define the relative weight or scope of these conditions, the Court's task was to chart that legal territory itself. Given the extremely vague language in the EC Treaty – for example, "all measures having equivalent effect" – the ECJ was not just settling disputes between the Commission and a Member State over the meaning of the text. Its decisions also determined which domestic interests would begin to experience the costs of adjusting to the agreements their governments consented to (Maduro 1998). Even in a country, such as Germany, that strongly favored economic integration, specific firms would begin to experience the costs of adjusting to the new legal environment.

Table 3.1 Policy and member state distribution of infringements

	ÖS	*DE*	*DK*	*SW*	*FI*	*NE*	*BE*	*LX*	*FR*	*IT*	*GR*	*PO*	*ES*	*IR*	*UK*	*Total*
Administrative matters	0	3	0	0	0	1	11	1	2	0	1	1	3	0	0	23
Budget isssues	0	6	2	0	0	2	5	0	3	7	2	1	3	1	2	34
Economic & monetary affairs	2	0	0	0	0	0	4	0	3	1	3	1	2	0	1	17
Internal market	17	56	9	3	1	13	49	11	105	82	46	10	24	13	11	*450*
Customs union & indirect taxation	1	8	5	2	0	5	11	3	16	15	18	8	8	8	6	114
Competition	0	1	2	0	0	1	4	0	6	10	3	5	1	2	2	37
Financial issues and taxes	0	0	1	0	0	0	4	0	4	7	1	0	0	4	0	21
Employment & social affairs	4	18	2	0	1	6	40	11	27	18	17	1	10	3	3	161
Aariculture	0	17	1	0	0	5	1	3	23	41	39	2	6	5	11	154
Transport	0	6	1	0	0	3	7	3	9	16	10	8	6	2	2	73
Energy	0	1	0	0	0	0	0	0	1	0	1	0	0	0	0	3
Trade policy/foreign affairs	0	1	0	0	0	1	0	0	4	0	8	1	0	1	1	17
Development	0	0	0	0	0	0	0	0	0	1	1	0	1	0	0	3
Fisheries	0	0	5	2	1	7	5	5	15	3	3	2	7	6	9	65
Environment	0	2	1	0	0	1	3	3	6	1	2	1	1	3	3	25
Legal questions	0	0	0	0	0	1	0	0	1	0	0	0	0	0	0	3
Business policy & tourism	0	0	0	0	0	0	0	0	0	0	0	0	1	0	0	1
Industrial policy	1	0	0	1	0	0	0	0	0	1	2	0	0	0	0	4
Justice	0	0	0	0	1	0	0	0	1	0	0	0	0	0	0	2
Statistics	0	0	0	0	0	0	0	0	0	0	2	0	1	0	0	3
Total	24	119	29	8	4	46	144	34	226	203	159	41	74	48	51	1,240

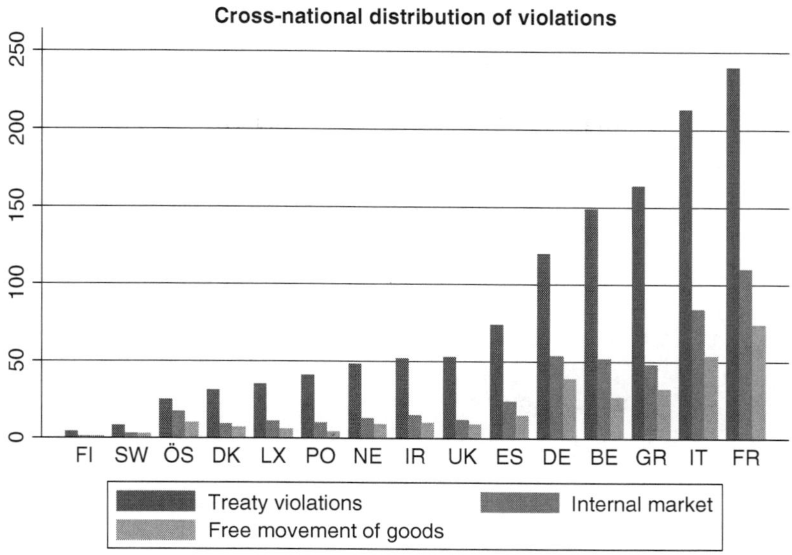

Figure 3.4 Cross-national distribution of infringements within the single European market.

According to Miguel Poires Maduro's masterful exegesis of ECJ case law in this area, the Court did not seek a completely deregulated economic space when it placed national regulations under suspicion for possible discriminatory behavior. Rather, through a series of rulings, the Court eventually established a doctrine of "majoritarian activism" (Maduro 1998). Through successive decisions related to Articles 34 and 35, Maduro argues that the Court was fulfilling its role as the protector of the EC Treaty and preventing protectionism by attempting to *harmonize* regulatory standards based on the practices that existed among a majority of the Member States.

The Court's first attempt to clarify the infamous language of "all measures having equivalent effect" in Articles 34 and 35 occurred in *Statistical Levy*.[11] In one of its first actions under Article 258 to enforce the EC Treaty against Member States, the Commission opened proceedings against Italy for assessing a level of ten lire per every hundred kilograms of imported goods in order to finance the gathering of trade statistics. Despite the clearly *de minimis* nature of the Italian charge, the Court ruled that:

> "…any pecuniary charge, however small and whatever its designation and mode of application, which is imposed unilaterally on domestic and foreign goods by reason of the fact that they cross a frontier, and which is not a customs duty in the strict sense, constitutes a charge having equivalent effect…"

The Court would attack not only national measures that were clearly discriminatory, but also all theoretically possible obstacles to the free movement of goods. The doctrine of attacking all possible measures was later confirmed by the Court's decision in *Dassonville*, which boldly stated, "All trading rules enacted by the Member States which are capable of hindering, directly or indirectly, actually or potentially, intra-Community trade are to be considered as measures having an effect equivalent to quantitative restrictions."[12] The Court not only conflated the difference between national measures that inhibit the access of products into national markets and the effect of national measures on the sale of these products once they arrived. It also assumed the powerful role of determining when those national laws placed an undue burden on foreign producers (Weiler 1999: 361–362). Thus, on the basis of these early decisions, one would expect that the Court's task was to slowly dismantle national rules that prohibited free trade within Europe and, thus, attack the rules that give unfair market advantages to national firms or industries.

Two subsequent rulings, however, qualified the extent to which the Court would force Member States to remove national regulatory measures in such areas as public health, consumer protection or the environment. First, in *Cassis de Dijon*, the Court ruled that Germany's desire to protect the public health of German consumers was legitimate, under Article 36 of the Treaty, but could be achieved through less intrusive means than banning all liquors below a certain minimum level of alcohol, such as through labeling.[13] Thus, as the Court famously stated: "There is no valid reason why, provided that they have been lawfully produced and marketed in one of the Member States, [products] should not be introduced into any other Member State," thus establishing the doctrine of mutual recognition.

The doctrine of mutual recognition is based on a proportionality test. The decision in *Cassis* did not necessarily imply that products manufactured according to "the lowest common denominator" would be permitted to enter national markets. Member States could retain their regulatory measures as long as the regulation did not "disproportionately" discriminate against other Member States' goods; those goods would be allowed entry if the exporting state's regulations met the technical standards of the targeted state. The Court is not primarily concerned with removing national regulatory obstacles simply for the sake of deregulating the internal market. Rather, it takes into account standards employed by a majority of other Member States and then determines whether the national standard under suspicion is stricter than those employed by other Member States accomplishing the same regulatory goal. As Maduro (1998: 68) makes clear, the Court's primary interest is the development of a *harmonized*, not deregulated, European market:

> The lack of harmonization of national rules places a burden on economic agents in the extra costs of having to comply with more than one set of rules. This impedes the achievement of some of the essential aims of an integrated market, such as economies of scale and lower prices. The problem

is not the burden with the regulation imposed *per se* on economic agents, it is the burden which derives from the existence of more than one regulation.

Thus, even when an EU directive would limit the free movement of goods, the Court tolerated such measures.[14] The Court's willingness to allow some national forms of protection was confirmed in the *Sunday Trading Cases*, whereby the Court found that a British law forbidding certain retail sales on Sundays was not discriminatory *and* could be justified as a legitimate state interest.[15] In its famous *Keck* decision, the Court even retreated slightly from its earlier decisions in *Dassonville* and *Cassis*: "Contrary to what has previously been decided," national regulatory measures that are applied irrespective of national origin to products from within the EC are lawful, "provided that those provisions apply to all affected traders operating within the national territory and provided that they affect in the same manner, in law and in fact, the marketing of domestic products and those from other Member States."[16]

The review of legal doctrine associated with the free movement of goods shows several important items regarding noncompliance in the EU. First, neither Germany nor France anticipated the ECJ would have the power to overturn national regulations. Second, as the ECJ and Commission started to construct the legal basis for the single market, the doctrine of mutual recognition would lie at its center. The ECJ's goal was not to remove or weaken national regulatory standards. Instead, only those practices that disproportionately achieved a commonly accepted policy goal faced the threat of being overturned. Those regulations that provided an unfair advantage to specific firms, based on qualitative requirements on products produced, marketed or distributed in a country, would come under scrutiny. In both the cases of the Beer Purity Law and restrictions on videocassettes in France, uncompetitive industries attempted to restrict competition by controlling specific markets based on taste. The former would not survive legal scrutiny, while the other would, but not for the reasons some scholars suggest.

Beer in Germany and film in France

Over the past thirty years, Germany has often clashed with the European Commission over the purpose and legality of its regulations related to manufactured items and the means by which they are sold. Some argue that since Germany has the largest economy in Europe, economic actors have significant financial incentives to develop their products according to Germany's practices and traditions. Moreover, if Germany plays a central role in the European integration process and, because of its power, is able either to influence the decision-making process of the European Commission or to avoid prosecution by the Commission entirely, then not only should the number of infringements Germany commits be comparatively low, but also the number of times those infringements are referred to the Court of Justice for settlement should be low.

Comparison with fourteen other Member States of the EU, however, shows that only France and Italy have infringed in the area of the free movement of goods more often than Germany. Approximately one-fifth of these German infringements underwent the judicial process, which is a comparatively smaller proportion than in cases involving many other Member States. Only six of 39 infringements were referred to the European Court of Justice for settlement between 1978 and 2002. This record shows that Germany generally settles many of its suspected infringements quickly. This is one indicator that most of the violations it commits are of a sufficiently low cost that they do not generate much opposition from domestic groups, especially in light of the economic and political gains Germany receives by complying with the EC Treaty. This was not the case, however, with the Commission's attempts to get Germany to repeal the *Reinheitsgebot*, or Beer Purity Law.

One key advantage German breweries had over their competitors was the restriction on what type of beverage could be sold as "beer." After the ECJ's ruling in *Cassis de Dijon*, one of the first cases to emerge on the European Court of Justice's docket in the area of the free movement of goods dealt with the *Reinheitsgebot* for beer in Germany. The Beer Purity Law stands as one of the oldest regulations in the world regarding the content and marketing of food and other consumable products. The original law dates to 1516 and Archduke Wilhelm IV of Bavaria, whereby all beer brewed in Bavaria could contain only malted barley, hops, yeast and water, and nothing more.[17] In 1952, and again in 1976, the *Reinheitsgebot* became codified federal law under the *Biersteuergesetz*.[18] Under Article 9, all beer produced and marketed in Germany was required to have these four ingredients. Furthermore, under Article 10, although any beer imported from outside of Germany would be permitted to enter the German market, it could not be marketed to the German public as "beer" unless it contained only these four ingredients.[19]

In the early 1970s, the European Commission attempted to begin the harmonization of laws related to the free movement of foodstuffs within the Community. The draft Brewing Directive proposed the inclusion of more than these four ingredients in the marketing of beer. According to Simon Bulmer (1986), the usual actors and institutional linkages worked in Germany in order to reject this draft directive. Interest groups mobilized within the brewing industry to form an "action committee" that led public opinion against the draft directive. In addition, the Bundesrat raised its opposition to the planned directive, given the plethora of small breweries in Germany. Partly as a result of all this national opposition, the draft directive was taken off the EC's agenda.

Through this type of political mobilization, we observe the beginnings of growing opposition to European integration as some sectors experienced the pain of economic adjustment coming from Brussels. Although Germany had obtained a temporary reprieve from harmonization imposed from above through European legislation, the European Court of Justice and the Commission increasingly assumed responsibility for maintaining the engine of economic integration. Because of economic crises and increasing protectionist policies among Member States in the early 1970s, EC officials feared that the goal of establishing a common market was in jeopardy. Therefore, when another opportunity arose to assert the importance of EC law and the development of a common market, the ECJ and the Commission seized it. One unintended consequence of European economic integration was the reorganization of national interest groups to advocate their policy goals at the EU level and cooperate transnationally (Sandholtz 1993).

In 1982, a French exporter of beer, *Brasserie du Pêcheur,* notified the Commission that Germany had fined its German distributor under the *Biersteuergesetz* for importing beer without paying the necessary duties that are assessed on alcoholic beverages that are not truly beer. Frequent administrative actions in Germany led Brasserie to discontinue all exports of French beer. Once the Commission was notified, it initiated Article 257, or infringement procedures, against Germany. The Commission issued a Formal Letter of Notice and then a Reasoned Opinion to the German government, both of which went unanswered. Finally, in 1984, the Commission brought Germany before the European Court of Justice for settlement.

This case reached the Court's tribunal for numerous reasons. First, the law was clearly protectionist, at least in the eyes of the Commission. In its case before the ECJ, the Commission argued: "The Beer Purity Law's only purpose is to maintain the current structure of the German brewing industry and to protect it from competition from other Member States." In 1986, imported beers marketed under the Reinheitsgebot accounted for only 1 per cent of total German consumption of beer. Germany has always possessed a strong trade advantage in beer exports (see Figure 3.5).

Total imports of beer have always lagged behind exports from EU Member States, enjoying a strong favorable balance of trade. In fact, the German balance in trade reflects Germany's overall trade with the European Union. German imports *and* exports to and from the EU constitute 50 percent of Germany's total foreign trade (see Figure 3.2). Therefore, one would expect that Germany would comply more often than not, given its interest in an expanding European market. Overall, therefore, the German economy benefitted as predicted by government negotiators. And integration was a net positive for the entire economy. But most of the costs would be borne by those small sectors that were not competitive.

Besides the health justification for the *Reinheitsgebot*, the Commission was questioning whether this law was effectively preventing the free entry of beers brewed in other Member States. Opposition by the Länder, in particular from Bavaria, was also fierce. In a series of articles that appeared in the *Süddeutsche Zeitung* between 1983 and 1987 during the court process, Minister President Franz Josef Strauß of the Christian Social Union sought to protect not only the hundreds of small breweries in Bavaria, but also German consumers, from beer of a supposedly lesser quality. Through Strauß's efforts, popular opposition to compliance grew. By 1985 most Germans not only became aware of the legal dispute, they were adamantly opposed to the Commission's demands.

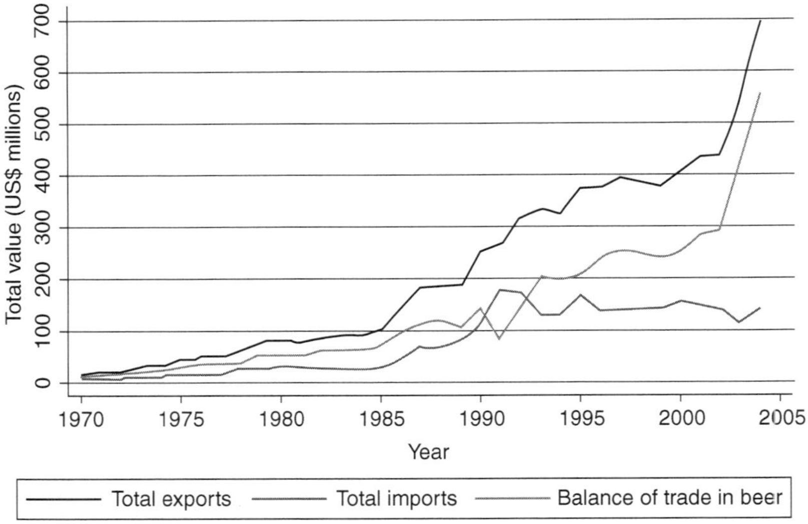

Figure 3.5 German beer trade with its EU partners.
Source: OECD

They perceived that a traditional element of German national culture was under attack by unelected bureaucrats and judges in Brussels and Luxembourg, respectively. Combined with opposition from the Länder governments, public opinion emerged to strongly oppose compliance with the Commission's demands.

Because the *Reinheitsgebot* originated in Bavaria, it is not surprising that opposition to changes in the federal law was fiercest there. The Beer Purity Law had stood for ages and served as the marker of high-quality German beer for centuries. Bavaria was also, however, experiencing a significant decline in the size of its brewing sector during the 1970s and 1980s that continues to this day. As a result of both European and international economic pressure, the number of breweries in Bavaria has been declining rapidly. Between 1956 and 1980, the number of breweries shrunk from over 1600 to just over 900. Although other Länder were also experiencing some decline in this sector, the condition was nowhere as severe as in Bavaria.[20] In addition, Bavaria has always possessed the highest number of small, family-run breweries with less than twenty employees. These small family breweries relied on the *Reinheitsgebot* not only to protect them from cheaper, more diverse varieties of beer from outside Germany. The purity law also served as a hallmark of their industry, distinguishing their products from the mass-produced beers of large, consolidated brewing companies. Thus, while the Commission's investigation challenged powerfully entrenched norms of how beer should be marketed and produced, powerful economic incentives existed as well, mainly in Bavaria, to delay compliance with EU law.

The vocal opposition in Bavaria, the largest and most powerful *Land* in Germany, was amplified by their access to political allies in Bonn. From the point at which the infringement was detected to the onset of the settlement process, Germany was governed by a coalition of the Christian Democratic Union and the Free Democratic Party, under the chancellorship of Helmut Kohl. In addition, the CDU had a controlling majority in the Bundesrat. Strauß could expect strong support from the national government for his position *vis-à-vis* the Commission. Because Chancellor Kohl was a strong supporter of European integration, he hesitated to allow infringements of EU law to delay the consolidation of the European market. In fact, the numerous non-tariff barriers to the free movement of goods that prevent the completion of the single market motivated Kohl and the Commission, under Jacques Delors, to move European integration forward through the Single European Act (Moravcsik 1991). Yet he could not ignore the growing opposition to compliance from his powerful allies.

The arguments that Minister-President Strauß made about why such protections of the German consumer were necessary paralleled those used by the government. The government in Bonn defended the law on the basis that it was protecting the public health and safety of its citizens.[21] First, the German government argued that any imported beer that did not meet the criteria set under Article 9 of the BStG would contain additives and thus be subject to the rules set out in the Law Concerning the Trafficking of Food Stuffs, Tobacco Products, Cosmetics and Other Consumer Goods, or *Lebensmittel- und Bedarfgegenständegesetz* (LMBG). According to the LMBG, §11, it is prohibited to market or sell any food product with additives that have not been previously authorized by the government. According to the German government, the prohibition of additives under the BStG existed to protect the health of German consumers. One core aspect of the German government's argument was that marketing a product as "beer" that did not conform to the *Reinheitsgebot* would mislead consumers into believing that the product did not contain additives and might therefore be harmful to their health. Since all beers that met these criteria could be marketed and sold in Germany, there was no violation of Article 34 of the EC Treaty.

While not fully discounting the desire of the German government's goal to protect the health of German consumers, it was also protecting the beer industry from competition from products within its industry in other countries. Through increased trade specialization, firms can develop niche markets that protect them from significant international trade pressures. In this case, however, the market niche German beers had, especially those produced by small and medium-sized firms, resulted from national regulatory protections. German beers would not face increased economic pressure based necessarily on prices, but on taste, if the purity law was lifted. Competition based on taste can either be vertical or horizontal. When consumers choose among products that differ according to contents but are still basically the same product, there is horizontal competition. Vertical competition exists when products compete over quality while using the same ingredients. In effect, the Beer Purity Law was restricting all competition to the vertical and disallowing any along the horizontal dimension. Through the Beer Purity Law, the German government, in effect, was attempting to maintain a major market advantage for domestic breweries, while using consumer health protection as a legitimate excuse.

Unsurprisingly, the Court rejected Germany's claims on several grounds. It conceded that, in the absence of EC legislation, Member States could place restrictions on the free movement of goods as long as the rules were proportionate to the aim being achieved, as defined in its earlier rulings. According to the Court, however, in this case the goals of protecting the consumer could be achieved equally effectively through less restrictive practices. First, under the principle of mutual recognition, if a specific additive was judged to be safe in another Member State and allowed to be included in the production of beer, an outright ban would be unnecessary. Moreover, Germany did not provide any scientific evidence that the additives included in foreign beers endangered the public's health.[22] Second, Germany argued that any importation of beer from other countries under such a label would confuse consumers. However, the Court argued that "consumers' conceptions are likely to vary from one Member State to another and to evolve in the course of time within a Member State. Hence, the legislation of that state cannot crystallize certain national consumer habits so as to consolidate an advantage acquired by national industries in the state of concern to comply with them. Secondly, such a generic designation may not be restricted to products manufactured in accordance with the rules in force in that Member State."[23]

As the Court's ruling states, the arguments Germany made to defend the Beer Purity Law were hardly plausible. The federal government's arguments would not pass any rigorous test of reasonableness. It was clear that the government decided to defend the case to protect a declining economic sector. The small and medium-sized breweries bore most of the costs associated with allowing other beers to be marketed in Germany on equal regulatory grounds. More beer imports, marketed on equal grounds with other beers, would eliminate their comparative advantage in the German beer market. The ability of other beer importers to market their beer in Germany as "beer," even though they were suspected of being of a "lesser" quality than native beer, would have the same effects as if there were a sudden supply shock. For the German consumer, this would also bring prices down significantly, especially since small and medium-sized firms could not produce enough to meet German demand. With over 60 million consumers of beer in Germany, the costs savings were significant, but diffused across the population. Germans would also have easier access to a variety of beers produced elsewhere in the EU. The small increase in beer imports after the Beer Purity Law decision indicates that some parts of the German market's demand for foreign beers was not being met because of the *Reinheitsgebot*. However, once these products were allowed in, demand appears to have become satiated and the amount of beer being imported into Germany leveled off (see again Figure 3.5). Thus, although the costs were high and concentrated on a specific sector of the economy, they were only over the short term.

Not only were the costs concentrated, but the political opposition as well. Although the small and medium-sized breweries were spread across West Germany, they were concentrated in Bavaria and in other regions with heavy CDU presence. With powerful allies such as Minister-President Strauß, the industry knew their interests could not be ignored. Small and medium-sized enterprises always were a core constituency of Christian Democratic parties in Germany. Even in the face of such a strong supporter of European integration as Helmut Kohl, the German government could not ignore the impacts immediate compliance and reform of the Reinheitsgebot would have on the German beer industry.

As a result of the Court's decision, both the *Biersteuergesetz* and the Lebensmittel- und Bedarfgegenständegesetz (LMBG) required significant changes. Three years after the Court's decision, the Federal Ministry for Youth, Family, Women and Health published a new "Bierverordnung," or beer regulation, that now permitted the import of beer with additives as long as it possessed a label written in German detailing all ingredients. Beer importers from other Member States were required to obtain a special license to import beers that contained additives that were not on a pre-approved list.

Despite continuing major opposition across Germany, especially in Bavaria, an almost 500-year-old law was changed approximately three years after the Court's decision. Yet the strategies that Germany devised to comply with the ECJ ruling proved insufficient. The beer regulation of 1990 continued to receive scrutiny from the European Commission.[24] In 1990, an additional infringement procedure was initiated against Germany that targeted Paragraph 47A of the LMBG, which placed additional cumbersome regulatory procedures on beers imported from outside Germany.[25] Consequently, the Federal Ministry for Health issued an additional regulation in cooperation with other ministries in 1993 that required Germany's labeling law to comply with the Labeling Directive passed in the meantime by the Council of Ministers.[26] According to the EC, the new regulation still discriminated against beer imports by forcing only non-German breweries to list ingredients. Although there were repeated meetings between German and EU officials, the government did not change the law until 1994, while the Commission initiated Article 258 proceedings against Germany, which could have led eventually to the application of economic sanctions. The label required all manufacturers from outside Germany to indicate whether a beer followed the guidelines of the *Reinheitsgebot*. The Commission argued that this label was still discriminating against beers from outside Germany. Finally, in December of 1995, the Bundesrat acted upon a regulation recommended by the Federal Health Ministry that permitted additional ingredients in products with less than 1.2 per cent alcohol by volume, and for these products to be marketed as beer as well.[27]

As domestic groups began to experience the effects of EU legislation, they seemingly realized that what happened in Brussels mattered materially. As the pace of European integration increased in the second half of the 1980s and 1990s, interest groups and trade associations began to reorganize themselves transnationally within Europe (Greenwood 1997, Greenwood *et al.* 1992). Despite the absence of any flood of imported beers, national lobbying groups such as the *Deutscher Brauer-Bund* began to form transnational lobbying organizations and alliances to place greater political pressure on officials in Brussels to protect their markets through supranational legislation. Pamela Camerra-Rowe (2004) documents this process as it occurred in the beer-brewing sector. As the brewing industry began to consolidate in Europe, the largest European brewing companies began to lobby Brussels directly rather than petitioning their national governments for harmonized taxes on alcohol products. Most importantly, in cooperation with breweries and food organizations across the EU, foods and drinks related to specific national traditions could also be protected. Under the European Parliament and Council Decision of 1997, national regulatory agencies were permitted to exclude certain additives from goods defined as "traditional foodstuffs."[28] Thus, in spite of efforts to harmonize foodstuff regulations at the European level, successful lobbying, combined with the interests of national governments themselves, led to the protection of German beer and other traditional national products, although European legislation was required to do somake this happen.[29]

The willingness and ability of the German beer- brewing industry to organize transnational alliances with other firms in other countries in the area of traditional foodstuffs shows how countries can change international law to suit their purposes and interests. But it is also extremely difficult and time-consuming. Debates over whether pure chocolate could contain vegetable fats or just cocoa butter paralyzed the EC Council for years. This dispute was also a proxy of a fight between Cadbury of the UK and Godiva and other Belgian chocolatiers over access and control of the European market for chocolate. The final directive approved by the Council would have a major impact on the future revenues for the industries in both countries (Bailer and Schneider 2006).

The case of the Beer Purity Law is an illustrative example of not only how effective interest groups can be who will have to bear the costs of noncompliance, but also how they can mobilize supporters when those costs are of a high magnitude. The German brewing industry was in an advantageous position. These breweries were located in parts of Germany where they could obtain easy access to sympathetic politicians.

The German beer case shows each of the mechanisms of my model of compliance at work. First, the costs of compliance were concentrated among a small group of firms. Trade data shows that the price shock that German breweries would face would subside over time. Still, fewer restrictions on beers from other countries would only increase the competitive pressures these breweries faced. In contrast, the benefits for German consumers were great, but dispersed across the population. The access that these breweries had in Germany to Länder governments and the national sentiments that the case evoked enabled this sector to pull the German federal government away from complying.

Their power to influence the German government was so great that the infraction almost led to economic sanctions imposed by the Commission. It is unlikely that Germany would have pushed noncompliance to the point of economic sanctions. It would not risk retaliation from other Member States and forgo the future gains of more market integration to please a declining economic sector of the German economy. Germany would not sacrifice European integration over a pint of beer. However, the Beer Purity Law case also shows how the groups that opposed compliance initially can delay compliance after the ECJ issues a ruling calling for change in state behavior. To bring Germany from noncompliance into compliance lasted almost ten years. In the meantime, other beer importers still faced discriminatory regulatory practices. Germany's reluctance to change the status quo to comply effectively is another powerful demonstration of how courts do not always succeed in generating policy change quickly or completely (Conant 2002, Rosenberg 1993).

French film and Funding

Much like the German beer industry, the French film industry faced a series of economic challenges after the signing of the Treaty of Rome. Exogenous changes in the economy, technology and consumer tastes led to declining returns. Like the German beer industry, the French film industry relied on national regulations to protect industries. The source of protectionism was not a direct tariff on imports but a form of "quality control." Namely, the *Fédération Nationale des Cinémas Français* relied on a French law that prohibited the selling of videocassettes of films still being shown in national cinemas. Several French and British firms then sued the national government in French courts for violating the legal principles behind the free movement of goods. After a preliminary reference, the ECJ found that the French regulation did not discriminate against EU imports. However, even though the French government won its case, we still see the political dynamics of noncompliance at work.

Like the German Beer Purity law, special support and protection for the arts in France dates back centuries. In 1635 Cardinal Richelieu created the *Académie Française*, whereby the French state would support and protect "official" art. Years later the French monarchy formed the *Comédie Française* that would serve as the "official" theater of France, both supporting and controlling all theater productions in France (Eling 1999). As a result, both domestic and international competitors who failed to achieve state recognition or support had much greater difficulty reaching the French audience. The strong, centralized support of the arts, as well as its creation and distribution by the state, has never really been challenged since then. The "exceptional" nature of French cultural policy is that the state attempted to define and shape it as various media developed over time. Art, in whatever form, was the direct expression of French identity. In contrast to popular films produced elsewhere, especially from Hollywood, the French government favored the filmmaker rather than the audience. Rather than for mass consumption, the French filmmakers and the government itself saw film as part of the arts, separate from the rest of society (Rollet 2005). As a result, the state and the industry would attempt to control the tastes of the French consumer and access to similar products within different media.

In contrast to the typical *dirigisme* of the French economy, however, the film industry emerged separately and autonomously from the state. Traditional conceptions of French-style capitalism place the French state at the center of economic policymaking, at least before recent institutional changes in the 1990s. Through coordinated investment strategies, large subsidies and protection for big businesses, the French state is intimately connected to French industry (Hall 1986, Schmidt 1996). But, because the film industry emerged independently from the state, it formed its own set of interest groups to coordinate lobbying activities. These *syndicats*, like any other lobbying group, aggregate the preferences of its members to achieve state support in the form of higher subsidies or protection from international competition. As a result, many of the classic elements of French *dirigiste* capitalism are not present. There are no state-mediating organizations that influence inter-firm relations. Industry and finance are separated from each other. And, most importantly, the state is not as interventionist in the French film industry as in other sectors of the economy. Instead, the film industry looks more like the disaggregated, pluralist form of interest group representation that exists in the UK. Thus, in *Cinéthèque SA*, it was not only the French state that sought to prevent EU imports, but the syndicates themselves, using French law to maintain a protectionist scheme.

In addition, in contrast to other artistic media, the French government's patronage of the film industry did not begin until well after the medium was invented, rather than parallel to its development as in the cases of painting and theater. France claims it was first in creating cinema and that Hollywood "copied" the structure of the French film industry.[30] Until the 1920s France was the leading film-producing country in the world, with the industry lying mainly in the hands of Pathé and Gaumont studios. However, its pre-war decline was mainly of its own making. The First World War played a significant role in the stagnation of French cinema in comparison with the United States. But, more importantly, it was Hollywood's new ability to mass-market films that Americans (and Frenchmen) wanted to see, as well as a lack of faith in the long-term profitability of cinema, that led Pathé and Gaumont to sell their film stock factories and production companies to the United States (Hayward 2000).

Patronage of the film industry did not start until 1944, with the creation of the *Institut des Hautes Etudes Cinématographiques* (IDHEC) under the Vichy government, and continued under the *Centre National de la Cinématographie* (CNC) in 1946. The CNC was a public body under the direction of the Ministry of Culture and Communication. It was mainly responsible for the funding and financial support of film production and distribution at that time. Most of the French film industry is funded through a tax on box-office revenues, or the *Taxe Spéciale Additionnelle*. In effect, successful films, mainly American ones, subsidize the production of French films. Public support from the French budget itself comes in the form of the *compte de soutien*, which itself is partly derived from a special tax on television companies. While France provides generous subsidies to the industry, these subsidies averaged only about 3 percent of the total annual budget of the Ministry of Culture from 1975 to 1991 (Eling 1999: 11). But, aside from strong support of the production of French industries, the organizational structure of French industrial representation is of the classic *syndicat* variety, enabling them to put direct pressure on the government for protection.

As American films grew in popularity both in the US and France in the early 20th century, they began to push French films out of the cinemas. The drive towards *auteur* cinema, for which most of French industry is known and celebrated, may have been driven by market forces as much as it reflected a national commitment to the fine arts. In light of competition for mass audiences and film production budgets on a scale most French firms could not match, both the French state and filmmakers redirected more of their funding activities to *auteur* cinema. As a result, the French government, together with the industry, was attempting to fill a niche in the film market that would be less exposed to international competition, particularly from the United States, and, therefore, to expand the amount of choice for French consumers. Since the French government could not control what films France imported, the more probable explanation for why France chose not to comply is based on the political power of the cinema syndicate.

The origins of the *Cinéthèque SA* case share some similarities with but also differ from those of the Beer Purity Law case in important ways. First, like German breweries, the French cinema was again experiencing some decline in revenues in the 1970s and 1980s. Film imports, mainly from the United States, challenged French-made films at the box office. The French state attempted to protect France from film imports through a series of trade agreements with the US, specified a quota for French films in national cinemas, and attempted to use co-production strategies to counter the influence of American imports (Hayward 2000: 200–202). None of these strategies would stem the decline. French audiences became smaller, especially as ticket prices rose in the 1980s (ibid.). The democratization of the arts led to a growing segmentation of the market for movies. Finally, new technologies, such as television and the videocassette recorder, led to greater competition for the Frenchman's leisure franc. It was only a matter of time before parts of the French film industry would seek to retain the economic protections that were available.

In *Cinéthèque SA*, the core issue was a French law that delayed the entry of videocassettes of all films into the French market until they had had their full run in the cinemas. The case emerged slightly differently from that of the German Beer Law. In the latter case, a French beer exporter notified the Commission that a German regulation unfairly and disproportionately discriminated against its exports to the German market, which triggered the compliance process under Article 258. In the case of *Cinéthèque SA*, a group of private firms sued a *syndicat* of national cinemas, the *Fédération Nationale des Cinemas Français* (FNCF), in French courts for violating EU law. Glinwood Films Limited had produced the film *Furyo*, one of the first successful box-office Japanese films produced in the English language.[31] Glinwood licensed the rights to show the film in theaters to *AAA SA*, which was granted a license to show the film in theaters in June 1983. In October 1983 *Cinéthèque SA* obtained the exclusive rights from Glinwood and AAA to distribute the film in videocassette form in Belgium, France and Switzerland. Immediately, the FNCF obtained an order from the French government for *Cinéthèque SA* to immediately cease and desist the distribution of videocassettes of the film under Article 89 of French Law no. 82-652 of July 1982.

The French law stated that no cinematographic work can be simultaneously shown in cinemas and be distributed in the form of a recording for private use to the public. Distribution of recordings was limited to a period between six and eighteen months after the film was granted a license to be shown in public theaters, or after the film was granted a performance certificate. *Cinéthèque SA* sued the FNCA in March 1984 in the Tribunal de Grande Instance, Paris, in order to have the decree lifted.[32]

In contrast to the German Beer Purity Law, this case did not result from an investigation by the Commission under Article 258. Instead, the French tribunal referred the case to the ECJ under Article 267 for a preliminary decision regarding a conflict between EU and French law. The plaintiffs claimed that the French law violated Articles 36 and 66. According to them, their inability to sell videocassettes within a specific time interval prevented them from selling goods in France that were legally produced and sold in all other Member States. In turn, the French government defended the law on several grounds. First, the law did not apply to *exports* of videocassettes of licensed films by French firms. If the police had mistakenly seized them, the law was misapplied. Second, the French government argued that the law was part of a larger body of law related to fostering the French film industry. Part of the revenues of box-office ticket sales was the primary means by which the production of French films was subsidized. Moreover, cinematic activities fell under the exceptional clause in that the law was justified on the grounds of legitimate public policy. Mere contractual arrangements between film producers and videocassette distributors would not be sufficient, given the market power of the latter, argued the French government.

The Commission came to the same conclusion. While the Commission disagreed with the French government and argued that the French law did restrict the imports and exports of goods lawfully made in other Member States, it agreed that the cultural purpose of the law fell under one of the exemptions located within Article 36. As long as the law did not exclude other films disproportionately, that it applied to French and EU products equally, and that it was an appropriate means to achieve the stated goal, the French law on videocassette production could remain in place.

The ECJ perceived the defendant and government's claims as also having merit. First, the ECJ dismissed the claim that the marketing of videocassettes constituted a service. The Court then turned to the issue of whether the French law restricting the time period by which videocassettes could be sold violated the principles behind the free movement of goods. In their initial comments, the Court believed that disparities in intra-EU trade did emerge because of different videocassette licensing systems across the EU; in that no other national system restricted videocassette production and distribution to as long as eighteen months, and the average in the rest of the EU was six months. Yet the Court found that the purpose behind the law, the fostering of national culture through film, was a legitimate activity under EU law.[33]

The *Cinéthèque SA* case shares many features with the Beer Purity Law case in Germany in terms of how a "losing" industry would bear most of the costs of European integration. First, the French film industry never received direct protections under the EC Treaty. At the intergovernmental meetings that led to the Treaty of Rome, French officials did not secure significant protections for the industries that would most be affected by increasing trade. Most of the benefits of the Treaty and future economic integration went to the largest sectors of France's economy, manufacturing and agriculture. Very few to no provisions were placed in the Treaty to protect import-competing industries. The French government acknowledged during intergovernmental bargaining that part of the price of agreeing to the Treaty of Rome was that some of its state-capitalist elements would face greater scrutiny. Yet, it was unaware that one of its key industries would experience hardship that was not explicitly a result of its policies of patronage. Specifically, the unintended consequence was the ability of private firms, whether French or non-French, to use the preliminary reference procedure in French courts to inquire whether a national law conflicted with EU law, which has supremacy.

Second, and more importantly, the French film industry experienced a variety of exogenous shocks since the Treaty was signed that affected the competitiveness of the industry. While French films never regained their box office supremacy in France after the 1920s, the industry limped along throughout the 1950s and 1960s. With the growing globalization of international media, new pressures on France's film industry began to appear. Once again, American films became more popular than French-made ones. Yet the data show that there was no serious threat to the production and protection of French films by the relative success of American films in French cinemas. Measured in terms of percentage of total box-office revenue, French films possessed relatively the same share of the total film market over the last thirty years (see Figure 3.6).[34] Although total revenues for French films in France are always less than for American ones, American films as a percentage of total box- office receipts remained relatively constant over time, and even decreased over time as French films gained a larger share of the French market.[35]

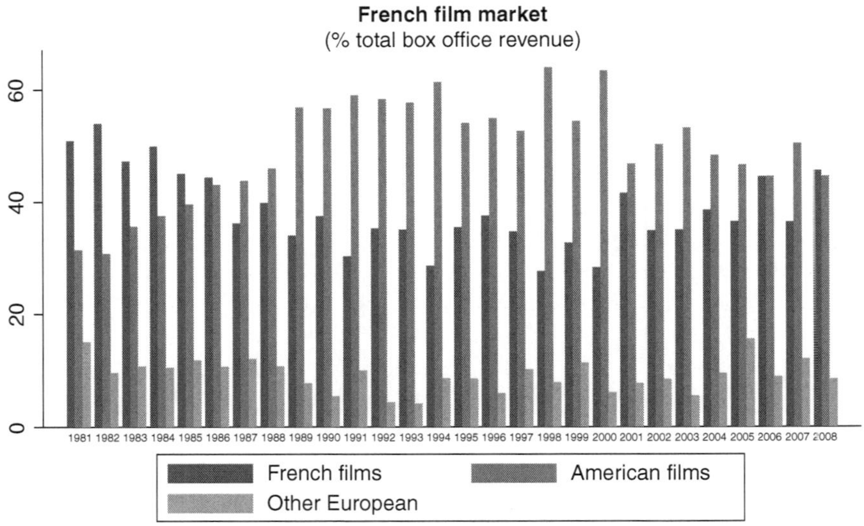

Figure 3.6 French film market revenues.
Source: CNC

From 1981 to 2008 total box-office receipts climbed from approximately €500 million to over a €1 billion, but attendance remained stagnant at an average of 240 million, falling from a high of almost 400 million in the 1950s. What the data show is that although overall attendance remained stagnant, receipts increased, mainly reflecting the increase in ticket prices over time.

Thus, the larger challenge to the French film industry was whether French people would spend their leisure and movie francs in the cinema or through the purchase of videocassettes for enjoyment in the privacy of their own homes. As a result, the *Cinéthèque* case had little to do with the production of French films. Instead, the case itself was about restricting the medium of the film experience and dealing with an exogenous technological shock that was common to the movie industry, and cinemas in particular, around the world.

The arrival of a new technology, the videocassette recorder, would have two effects. First, it was primarily a threat to the cinema industry, but not to the government's ability to raise revenue through the special taxation scheme. The arrival of the videocassette and subsequent pirating of films still running in theaters was a danger to the survival of France's patronage scheme if attendance went down even further. However, movie theaters were not the only source of revenue. Since the 1940s, France had succeeded in diversifying the sources of financing for the French film industry. Direct state aids, television fees and banks were also strong alternative sources of financial support. In addition, beginning in the 1970s, France attempted to foster its industry by arranging co-productions with other European countries, beginning with Italy. In the 1980s, under the Socialists, two new mechanisms of state financing were made available. First, the *avances sur recettes* are direct payments to new filmmakers of promise who produce films of quality, since the *soutien automatique* favors large, established film producers. Second, the Socialist government also created the *Société pour le financement du cinéma et de l'audiovisuel* or SOFICA, a financial group whereby a group of producers can invest up to fifty percent of taxable revenues into productions and receive a tax benefit as a result (Hayward 2000: 202–203). Data from the *Centre national du cinéma et de l'image animée* (CNC) shows that although attendance in national cinemas has been relatively stagnant since 1980, total funding by the government for French films increased from approximately €200 million in 1981 to €1.1 billion in 2007.[36] In addition, box-office sources of movie revenues decreased as a share of total state funding, even though there was no dip in box office receipts (see Figure 3.7).[37]

This partly explains the rise of some big-budget French films that successfully competed on theater screens worldwide (Gordon and Meunier 2001). Thus, the data show that neither the dominance of American movies on cinema screens *nor* stagnant ticket sales were threatening the French state as the chief patron of French cinema. Rather, the law was protecting French cinemas from another threat, the rise of new media technology.

What the French regulation on videocassette production did do was to limit when French consumers could enjoy their films on other media platforms.

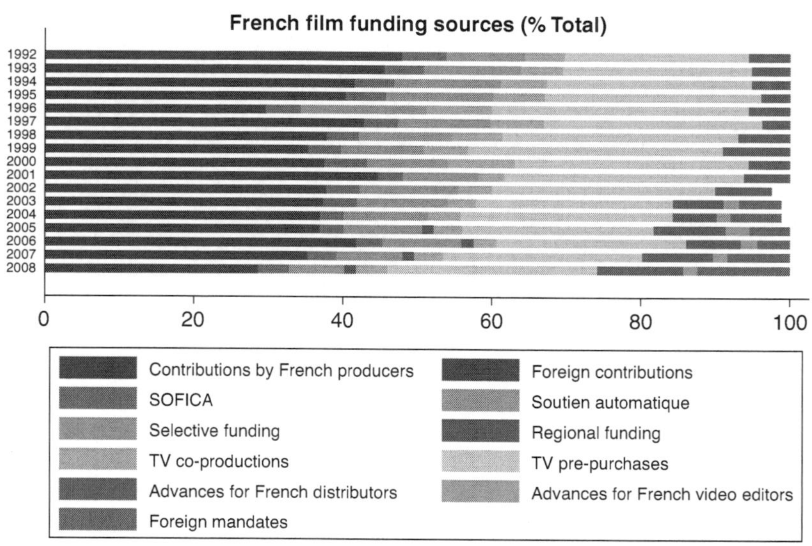

Figure 3.7 Public funding for French films.
Source: www.cnc.fr

The French government was not controlling the entry of foreign films *per se*. Rather, the law privileged the cinematic experience in movie theaters. Growing piracy and home video watching would undoubtedly affect ticket receipts and, therefore, the degree to which French filmmaking could be supported. In terms of overall film quality, part of the *auteur* film genre is also the experience of enjoying a film in a theater setting, rather than alone. French film watching is more of a communal activity in which the experience is to be shared. Thus, from the perspective of the French government, the law protected a certain type of film-watching experience, not French films from European or American competition.

Whatever the merits are to this argument, the primary purpose of the law, and the reason for litigation, was the impact it had on protecting French cinematic theaters from competition. The main victims, or losers, associated with the repeal of the French licensing law would have been French cinemas. If videocassettes of films appeared shortly after their theatrical release, the losses would be both high and concentrated for the members of this *syndicat*. The French state could absorb some of the losses if videocassettes of films were rapidly released. Moreover, consumers would benefit greatly from the repeal of the law. The price of watching a film would decline substantially, especially if the product appeared on the streets very soon after the film's theatrical release. If consumers could watch movies in their own private households sooner, and not even pay for the privilege, then cinemas across France would face serious economic losses. While these gains would be great, they would be distributed across the entire French population. In contrast, it was the French cinema groups that would bear most of the costs of the law's repeal.

Does the victory of the FCNA represent a case of the ECJ bowing to political pressure of a powerful Member State, as Garrett (1995) claims? Over time, the ECJ did start backing away from some of its more sweeping judgments of the past that sought the removal of many types of nontariff barriers to the free movement of goods. Before *Cinéthèque*, the Court had rarely upheld national regulations based on the controls listed in Article 36, such as public health, cultural, or other exclusions justified by the Treaty. This case was part of a slow reversal of the Court's doctrine of removing all types of national restrictions on the free movement of goods and services as laid down in *Dassonville*.[38] But, a close analysis of the case shows that while the French government did strongly prefer the law on cinema certifications to remain in place, it did not challenge a key interest of the government. Rather, the prime motivation for keeping the law in place was to protect the cinema *syndicat*.

Second, Garrett (1995: 179) provides little evidence that the law was protectionist of the French film industry. First, if it were, the Commission would have been expected to argue strongly for the repeal of the French law. Instead, the Commission sided with the French government by stating that purpose of the law conformed to EU law so long as it was not discriminatory, was proportional to the ends sought, and the goal could be justified. It was not a "clear violation of free trade." Second, the law did not protect the French film industry from international competition from other film producers. Rather, it was protecting the cinema or movie theater industry from *domestic* competition, namely VCRs and videocassettes. The French government welcomed all films to be shown on their film screens. While the French government bemoans the popularity of foreign films, especially those from Hollywood, their popularity is an important, although decreasing, element for future financing of French films.

Third, Garrett's analysis provides little justification for why the Court ruled in France's favor, or more precisely the cinema industry's. He argues, "The reason for the court's behavior is clear: it understood that protecting the domestic film industry was a 'no go' area for the French government … the ECJ knew that the French government would not abide by a decision to remove this trade protection (ibid.: 179–180)." But there is little evidence that the Court was interested in striking down this form of protection in its ruling. The result reached cannot also be its cause. Even if true, why would the Court decide to favor the French film industry and not the German beer industry? The German government provided just as many if not more signals that it would not comply with the ECJ's ruling, at least not immediately. Therefore, according to Garrett's theory, we would expect the Court to rule in favor of Germany in regards to the *Reinheitsgebot* and *not* in favor of France, indirectly, in the case of *Cinéthèque*. Garrett provides little insight how the Court decides which Member State's threats of noncompliance are more credible than another's.

Conclusion

In both the Beer Purity Law and French videocassette cases, the losses associated with European integration were high and concentrated in a small industry. As competitors with imports, firms in these industries faced serious economic adjustment costs as economic integration accelerated. The laws that came under legal scrutiny were those that gave firms or an industrial sector an unfair advantage in terms of quality. Many national laws became suspect if, rather than being outright forms of price support, they disproportionately discriminated against goods and services from other countries by giving them unfair qualitative advantages in the European market place.

In both the cases of the *Reinheitgebot* and *Cinéthèque*, the governments chose to fight on behalf of the groups most affected by trade liberalization. Both the small and medium-sized brewers in Germany and the French cinemas enjoyed special access to political institutions in their respective countries. The resonance of these industries in the national consciousnesses and cultural identities of each country helped motivate strong support from the rest of the population, especially in the case of Germany. In both cases the public good's framework explains why and where violations of EU law took place, even in two countries strongly supportive of European integration. The German Beer Purity Law also shows how governments can delay full compliance over time. Nevertheless, the German government eventually satisfactorily changed the legislative status quo. They favored the long-term gains of future integration over the short-term costs that EU legal integration in the area of the free movement of goods were producing. These problems would repeat themselves in the case of the direct state subsidies to industry as well, which is the focus of Chapter 4.

4 Stopping state rescues

Complying with EU state aid policy in Germany and the United Kingdom

Introduction

The previous chapter explores how losers, caused by European economic integration, lobbied their governments to refrain from complying with EU law. The absence of generous side payments at the negotiating table, exogenous changes in the European economy and technology, and more precise legal obligations all combined to bring the German and French governments into noncompliance. For both German beer breweries and French cinemas the costs of compliance were concentrated, while the benefits of complying with EU law were distributed across consumers in each country. These firms then used both institutional ties and appeals to national tradition to generate support from the general public to protect their industries.

Neither the German nor the French government wanted to sacrifice the long-term economic gains of cooperation to save French cinemas or small German breweries. Yet, in spite of the salience of these industries in the national conscience, the contributions these industries made to the overall national economy were quite small. Therefore, we should ask: do states comply even when core national interests are under attack? So far, the evidence is mixed (Panke 2010). Another core hypothesis is that governments comply most often when there is a high degree of legalization (Wolf 2005). Compared to other international regimes, the EU does secure higher rates of compliance. But even within the EU there are variations in degree to which a regime is legalized. And noncompliance still occurs. If so, what are the sources of it? Why are states reluctant to change the status quo, even though the law is clear and there are effective procedures to handle legal disputes, as well as strong monitoring and sanctioning mechanisms?

This chapter addresses these questions by examining noncompliance in two countries related to EU state aid policy. Preventing governments from subsidizing declining, uncompetitive industries has long been a central objective of EU law and policy. First, this was one of the EU's key goals of reducing state intervention in national economies. Second, state subsidies distorted the European market by giving unfair competitive advantages to specific firms or industries and, thereby, inhibiting complete market integration.

At the same time, there are strong incentives for governments to free ride. The Commission does not have the necessary resources to detect and prosecute all violations of the EU's state aid rules. Even though the Competition Directorate (DGIV) is one of the most powerful parts of the EU's bureaucracy, not only does noncompliance still occur, it also varies across the Member States. There is little doubt that the cross-national pattern in state aid violations is related to the different policy traditions of state support for industry or poor regions among the Member States. Yet, even in countries such as Germany and the UK, where state subsidies are not part of institutionalized policy traditions and there is strong ideological opposition to them, noncompliance still happens. However, we are least likely to expect noncompliance in these countries. In addition, despite very different political regimes and attitudes towards EU supranational authority, compliance eventually occurred in both countries, even when the ECJ ruled in favor of the British government.

The case studies of the German Landesbanken and the subsidies given to MG Rover show how governments eventually comply even when there is strong opposition to the EU's supranational authority. The levels of skepticism towards Brussels among both the Länder in Germany and the British government during the Thatcher years were both comparatively high. Noncompliance also happened for the same reasons as in the German beer and French cinema industries. First, neither the Landesbanken nor the British automobile industry secured protection during intergovernmental negotiations. Second, a strong competition policy, especially a robust anti-state-aid policy, developed and the Commission's powers in this area expanded without the careful supervision and assent of the Member States. Third, exogenous and unanticipated shocks to the economic sectors of both the German banking industry and British automobiles placed new fiscal pressures on them, or exacerbated old ones. Each of these sectors then obtained strong political support from political allies, despite the financial costs for the rest of national society. The benefits of saving both Westdeutsche Landesbank (WestLB) and other Landesbanken, or the German development bank system in general, and MG Rover, I argue, were concentrated. In contrast, the benefits of removing these unlawful subsidies were diffused across the German and British population. Yet, neither case was ultimately settled by the ECJ. Instead, both countries complied beforehand, because national support for the infringement was divided and future steps towards European integration were at stake.

State aid policy in the EU

Competition policy is one of the most supranationalized policies in the European Union. The Competition Directorate, also known as DGIV, has a broad scope of authority over Member State policies in a policy area of great national political sensitivity. The development of a rigorous state aid, or anti-subsidy, regime reflects many of the political dynamics associated with the establishment and functioning of the international institutions mentioned in Chapter 2.[1] The Member States did not anticipate the full consequences of the agreements they had made. The language used to deter unlawful subsidies was vague, which allowed the Commission and the ECJ to work together to create a stronger regime than the Member States intended. Finally, the Commission was responsible for enforcing the EC Treaty in order to produce the collective good of an undistorted single market. Without effective enforcement, each Member State would effectively free ride and the goals of European integration would not have been reached.

Neither the Member States nor the Commission expected such a strong policy regime to develop. When an EU competition policy was first emerging, most countries did not have a set of policies that prohibited either accumulated economic power among firms or state intervention in the economy. Most countries had some form of industrial policy. They used state funds to achieve regional or sector development or to rescue failing firms. The first elements of a policy to deter government subsidies appeared in Articles 92–94 of the EC Treaty (now Article 107 TFEU). These provisions sought to prevent national or subnational authorities from providing aid to companies that distorted competition. Numerous exceptions were included, such as aid to consumers, responses to natural disasters and, later, German financial assistance for the new Länder (Article 107(c) TFEU). The Council could also approve, by qualified majority voting, aid to promote development in regions with abnormally low levels of standard of living, high levels of unemployment, to encourage the development of specific economic activities, or to support cultural or historic preservation (Articles 107(a–e)).

The Treaty of Rome also laid out a series of strong enforcement measures in cases of illegal subsidies. First, under Article 108, all Member States must notify the Commission of all new aid, as it monitors all existing state aid programs. If notification is not given or the Commission finds that the proposed state aid program is not compatible with the Common Market, the Commission can order the business to return the aid to the state. If noncompliance continues, the matter is referred to the European Court of Justice, leading to additional fines if the national government does not comply. The EU Council may grant specific exemptions to the rules in a particular case by a unanimous vote. In contrast to Article 258, there are no clear provisions that allow either private EU citizens or other national governments to notify the Commission of suspected unlawful aid. Nevertheless, the state aid regime, and the EU's competition policy that is one of the most powerful legal regimes within the EU and among international institutions that address anti-trust issues.

Despite the legal strength of the regime, the provisions were rarely enforced until the 1980s. In the 1950s and 1960s state intervention in the economy was still a standard practice and an accepted notion among West European governments. In the 1970s recession and deindustrialization limited the Commission's interest in enforcing state aid rules. When economic integration again became a priority in the 1980s, with the drive to complete the single market, the Commission's enforcement efforts increased. In addition, there was a growing amount of EU case law that further clarified what qualified as state aid and the powers the Commission had in this area (Cini and McGowan 2009). Enforcement of state aid provisions was also given greater priority because of the strong political entrepreneurship of DGIV Commissioners Sir Leon Brittan and Peter Sutherland.

Preventing unlawful forms of state aid is an important part of constructing a single market where goods and services, as well as capital and people, are allowed to move freely. From the perspective of economic efficiency, state aid is not an appropriate expenditure of scarce resources. Interest groups or firms often use state aid to stay afloat, instead of those resources being reallocated to more productive areas of the economy. It can lead to rent seeking, whereby firms choose not to invest in new production strategies, further decreasing national competitiveness. In extreme circumstances, it can lead to corruptive practices between the government and its patrons (Spector 2009).

Proponents of state aid argue that it serves several important economic purposes. First, in some circumstances, state subsidies can lead to positive externalities. Investment in R&D, retraining of workers and corrective tax policies can lead to long-term growth in a particular region or industry. Second, it can be used to address problems of informational asymmetry, whereby firms with profitable innovations are unable to secure capital on the open market (Spector 2009: 186–187). Overall, however, assessing the net positive or negative impact of state aid is quite difficult. In light of this, the European Union's key focus is to declare state aid illegitimate if it distorts competition and trade within the EU.

The standard of proof that the Commission uses to identify which types of aid have the effect of distorting competition or trade is low. In *Phillip Morris*, the Court devised the criteria for the first time.[2] The Court ruled that if the state aid affected the production capacities of an enterprise, all other enterprises were affected by the unfair advantage given to the national firms and, thereby, this affected EC trade. Subsequent rulings, such as in *Tubeneuse*[3] and *Maribel*[4], stated that state aid could affect EC trade even if the firm's production was primarily for the domestic market and the assistance was of a minimum amount. And no market, no matter how locally specific, was immune to the possible distorting effects of state aid.[5] With such a low threshold for how state aid affects EC trade and the Commission's strong commitment to complete the single market, not many state practices would be immune from legal scrutiny.

Thus, analyzing the causes of noncompliance within the EU's anti-state-aid policy is a rich place to test this book's model of compliance behavior. The gains of state aid are concentrated among one or a few firms. Arguably, the costs of maintaining these programs could be either minimal or large in scope. According to standard economic theory, this leads to increased market inefficiency and costs to national taxpayers. This assumes that the aid does not lead to significant positive externalities, such as sustained consumer demand and economic growth in the region granted the aid. Whatever the balance turns out to be, the gains associated with receiving aid are concentrated, while the costs of providing it are diffused across the national population.

The EU breaks down state aid into several categories: agriculture, fisheries, horizontal and sectoral objectives, and transport. Horizontal aid refers to measures the government uses to spur economic growth directed towards the entire economy, such as research and development funds, training programs and general assistance to small and medium-sized enterprises. Sectoral aid includes assistance to specific industries, such as coal or steel. Germany leads the way in total state assistance, most of which is aid directed to the former East German Länder. The largest EU Member States, with the exception of Ireland, follow. Clearly, the largest states, measured in economic size, provide most of the state aid (see Figure 4.1).

Measuring noncompliance with EU state aid rules is a difficult enterprise. Since the Commission's goal is to reduce state aid in the EU, some measure compliance in terms of whether it declines over time (Blauberger 2009). Yet, that does not capture actual noncompliance. A government could still award small amounts of aid, but still violate the conditions when granting state aid. For example, in Figure 4.2, Austria awards a small amount of aid as a percentage of its gross domestic product, but fails to notify the Commission, as required under EU law, more often than other Member States which award more aid.[6]

One of the legal requirements Member States are obliged to follow is to notify the Commission of all ongoing and future state aid measures. Figure 4.2 compares the number of times a Member State failed to notify the Commission

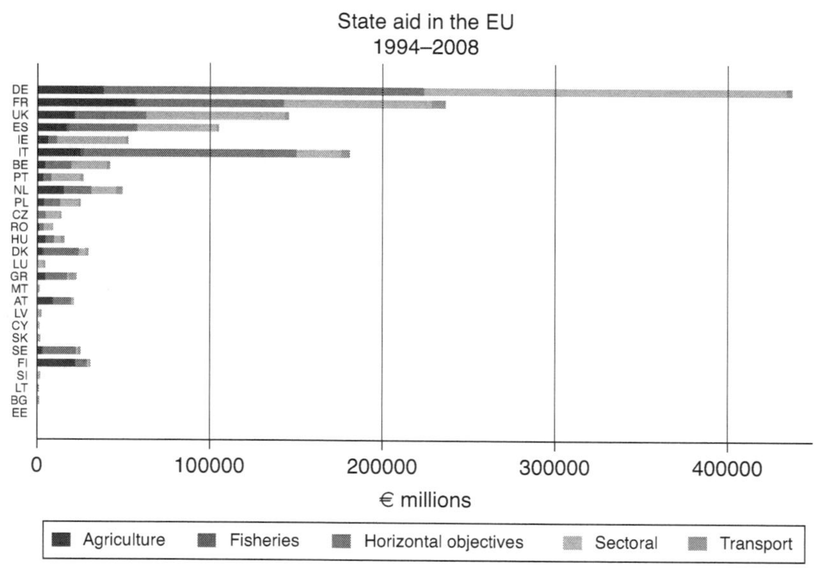

Figure 4.1 Cross-national distribution of state aid.
Source: European Commission State Aid Reports.

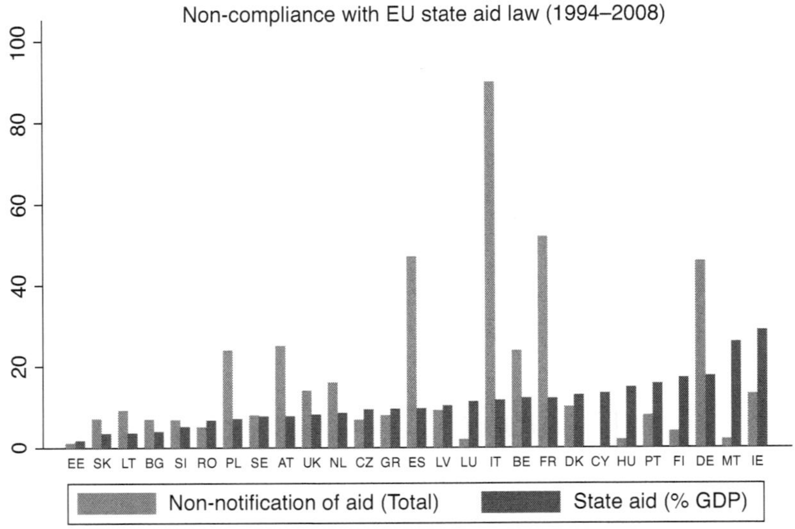

Figure 4.2 Violations of EU state aid law.
Source: EC State Aid Reports.

of a particular program with a country's state aid as a percentage of its gross domestic product. In the figure, we observe that Italy, Belgium and France, along with Germany, fail to notify the Commission most often. Violations of EU law and total state aid granted are weakly correlated with each other ($R^2 = 0.058$). The Commission is also empowered to decide whether the state aid measure is legal under EU law. If not, or if the decision of the Commission is negative, a Member State's government must retrieve the funds it awarded. Between 1990 and 1994, Italy led the way with twelve negative decisions, followed by Germany with nine, France with five and the UK with only three.[7]

Thus, the pattern of violations mirrors, to some extent, the cross-national patterns of noncompliance in others areas of EU law. Just as there is variation in determining which countries commit more violations of EU law than others, so is there variation in terms of notification and prosecutions of the rules related to EU state aid policy. Relative to the amount of state aid given, both Germany and the UK appear to comply at relatively equal, but high, levels. In both cases, the costs of noncompliance were concentrated among a small group of actors. However, because neither group could achieve broad national support for noncompliance, the cases were settled without an ECJ ruling. In fact, the firms that were receiving the illegal aid actually won their cases before the Court. Because the Rover and Landesbanken cases did not have broad political support among the general public and future steps towards integration would have been jeopardized by continued noncompliance, these cases were settled relatively swiftly.

Ending subsidies for German banks and British cars

State aid policy, or government subsidies to industry, is a policy area in which noncompliance is least expected in both Germany and the UK. In contrast to France's tradition of a *dirigiste* or "directed" economy, both countries provide significantly less direct forms of financial assistance to industry. In Germany, the philosophy of *sozialmarktwirtschaft*, or a social market economy, persisted for decades. Under this rubric, the state is tasked with ensuring markets function optimally, while the undesired distributive effects of markets are addressed through social welfare policies (Allen 1989, Smith 2001a). The Freiburg school of economic thought, born in the post-Nazi era and highly skeptical of the power of special interest groups, had strong aversions to the use of protectionism and special forms of state assistance.

Similarly, in the United Kingdom, there is a strong policy orientation towards little state interventionism in the economy. Along with the United States, the UK is seen as one of the most liberal market economies in the world. Especially during the Thatcher years, there was a strong commitment to deregulation, liberalization and privatization. In contrast to both Germany and France, there are no institutionalized ties or networks that bring the state and firms or industries together. In contrast, there is a highly decentralized form of business organization, which leads firms to lobby on their own and compete with others for protection (Hall and Soskice 2001, Schmidt 2002). Because of ideology and the absence of strong state–business connections, industrial policy as a strategy to grow or aid specific firms or economic sectors is almost nonexistent in the UK.

Given that both of these countries lack any established policy tradition of providing financial assistance to growing or struggling firms, it is unlikely that they would commit violations of EU state legal policy. Therefore, we might expect any aid that these countries do provide to a firm to be of great national importance. If so, then the governments seek to retain those policies and even refuse to comply with EU demands to end them. But we do not see that in the German or British cases. Despite Court rulings in favor of both the *WestLB* and the Rover Group, both countries complied in the early stages of the compliance process.

WestLB and the removal of loan guarantees

Although Germany does not possess a strong, coordinated form of financial assistance that targets struggling or growing industries, with the exception of those in the former East Germany, there are some key policies in place that give preferential treatment to some unique German financial institutions. Landesbanken, or development banks, were key to the redevelopment of German industry after the Second World War. And they operated in a unique German way. Rather than giving direct grants of financial assistance, they offered loans to both Länder governments on more generous terms than were available on the free market. These policies lasted for decades and created strong political supporters across the political spectrum in Germany. However, growing competitive pressures within the global financial industry led private, *domestic* German banks to notify the Commission of possibly illegal practices by the German government under EU state aid law. Over time, despite very strong opposition, the government changed the status quo and took small but significant steps towards changing the policy through liberalization of a protected sector of the German financial industry.

Germany is widely considered to have a different and unique model of capitalism. In contrast to the Anglo-Saxon model, the German system epitomizes the role of coordination across the various components of modern capitalism – firms, banks, labor, corporate governance and educational or training systems. Rather than market pressures being the primary forces shaping economic adjustment, noneconomic institutions and networks that link these different sectors shape adjustment patterns. The system of corporate finance in Germany is no different. German banks use their close connections to different segments of German industry to plan out long-term investment strategies while monitoring their management. The state remains at a distance. It only serves to provide the regulatory, legal and selective resources to guide negotiations between banks and large firms.

Many of these banks are characterized as "universal banks" in that they combine commercial and investment banking activities. Examples include Deutsche Bank, Commerzbank and Dresdner Bank, the three largest national commercial banks. But Richard Deeg (1999) shows how characterizing the entire sector as being composed mainly of these universal banks ignores the important diversity within it. Commercial banks sit alongside regional savings and cooperative banks. The saving banks, located at the Land level, provide long-term lending to individuals and small and medium-sized enterprises (SMEs) as well as to large-scale industry. The cooperative banks provide generally the same services but for specific segments of the German economy, such as farmers.

For decades these banks existed side-by-side and, although they were in competition with each other, they also participated in different niches of the lending market that enabled them to provide a stable source of investment capital for German firms. The savings bank sector consists of over 700 small, communal-based banks that provide both commercial services, such as savings accounts and other products for individual customers, and lending services for SMEs that follow the policy initiatives of local governments. These banks are owned in turn by the Landesbanken, or development banks, located at the state level. Ownership of the Landesbanken is shared between the Land government and the association of savings banks in that state, or *Girozentrale*.[8] As such, these banks are not entirely private, nor are they wholly owned subsidiaries of the state, but can serve both public and private customers.

The large, private commercial banks always perceived the special functions and privileges Landesbanken held as unfair because they held a competitive advantage in securing working capital. Beginning in the 1960s, increasing domestic and foreign competition led to the merger of local savings banks into the larger, more powerful Landesbanken, partially owned by state governments. Their larger size and the equity they accumulated over the years as savings banks allowed them to gain a greater share of the German lending market. Between 1972 and 1996, the largest private lending banks issued between 13 percent and 15 percent of all loans to firms. In contrast, the savings and cooperative banks accounted for almost 50 percent of all business loans.[9]

But they also held special legal advantages that enabled them to gain a growing share of that market. As Michael Smith (2001a) points out, the Landesbanken enjoyed three basic benefits not available to the commercial banks. First, they enjoyed unlimited liability by having the full financial guarantee of the state government. All depositors and creditors would face full compensation if their assets became at risk in the event of bank default. Second, because of this guarantee, these banks enjoyed higher market credit ratings and thus lower borrowing costs. Third, because these banks were owned partly by the state government and their priority was to lend to SMEs or other development objectives, there was far less concern about generating profits. The banks were more immune to demands of private shareholders to meet quarterly or short-term profit expectations than private banks were. Instead, these banks concentrated on obtaining a larger market share of the domestic lending market over the long term.

This hardly pleased the big commercial banks. For decades the Big Three, Deutsche Bank, Dresdner Bank and Commerzbank,[10] fought to remove these special privileges by appealing to the federal government, but always ran into strong political opposition. It was only when the large commercial banks complained to the European Commission about possible violations of EU law that they were able to obtain some relief.

Before discussing the specific origins of the *WestLB* case, it is important to point out who directly benefitted from the activities of the Landesbanken and, therefore, who faced the greatest losses if these special privileges were eliminated. First, the activities of the Landesbanken constituted one of the only forms of "industrial policy" in Germany. Although Germany does not have an institutionalized system of federal assistance for specific firms, or direct finance capital to selected firms, as in France, the Landesbanken serve as a key element of the German economic model. By providing long-term, low-cost loans, German firms are available to pursue the strategy of diversified quality production (Deeg 1999, Hall and Soskice 2001, Streeck 1992). Firms are then enabled to invest in valuable, but time-consuming, innovations in order to occupy specific market niches within a manufacturing sector. Stable sources of funds for investment enable companies to form and maintain the extensive apprenticeship programs needed to create a highly skilled workforce that is necessary for this type of production strategy. Thus, the removal of these loan guarantees, some people thought, threatened the German model of economic growth and strength.

But long-term investment in regional economies as well as in small and medium-sized enterprises is not the only function of these Landesbanken. They serve as key tools of state intervention in the economy, a role usually underestimated but one that Richard Deeg (1999) expertly documents. In the late 1960s and 1970s the government of North-Rhine Westphalia (NRW) faced the decline of its major industries, chiefly coal, steel, iron and heavy machinery. Because of technological change and growing international competition, the firms in this industry needed to start changing their production strategies. The Social Democratic government then in power collaborated with the Landesbank of North-Rhine Westphalia, Westdeutsche Landesbank (WestLB), to implement a set of policies to assist restructuring efforts. Through coordination between WestLB, industrial firms, the unions and the Land government, the industrial firms instituted strategies to reduce capacity and invest in new, diversified forms of quality production in specific niches of the steel market, such as retraining, job-creation programs and social assistance for unemployed workers (Deeg 1999: 129–133). As Deeg and others have illustrated, WestLB was a key tool in carrying out the Land's interventions in the regional economy.

Because of their mixed public–private nature, WestLB and other Landesbanken permitted the firms both to serve the development interests of their government owners and to have a strong presence in Germany's commercial banking sector. Through their quasi-independence from state governments, these Landesbanken obtained greater shares of the German lending market. However, the political nature of the Landesbanken should not be underestimated. First, Landesbanken acted as "housing banks" for the Land as much as independent development banks. They became the states' primary business partners by distributing public funds and handling the states' financial difficulties (Döring 2003). Because the state governments are part or full owners of the Landesbanken,[11] these governments could use these banks' commercial services at a significant discount compared to what they would get if they used fully independent, private banks.

In addition, if banks such as WestLB chose not to fulfill the policy goals of the Land's government, the banks' leadership would be replaced or its mission restated. The political party in power often shaped the bank's mission and activities. While SPD-controlled governments strongly supported state intervention in the regional economy, the CDU was always more skeptical of this role for the banks. When Ludwig Poullain assumed leadership of WestLB in the late 1960s, he moved, with the backing of the SPD government, to expand the bank's services into purchasing equity shares in large firms in order to better implement the state's development plans. The Land of North-Rhine Westphalia also supported the bank's strategy of expanding its international financial activities, mainly by placing state ministers on its administrative board (Deeg 1999: 137). Finally, whenever the president of the bank was suspected of engaging in unlawful or improper activities, as Poullain was in 1977, the state government could force that person to resign.

Why is it important to emphasize the public role of WestLB? First, as Richard Deeg shows, the Landesbanken are key elements in German industrial policy. While arguably the entire German economy benefits when firms are able to weather and adjust smoothly to changes in the international economy or technology, those gains are concentrated in particular economic sectors. Second, those economic gains are also concentrated at the regional level.[12] Third, these banks act at the behest of their government owners. Therefore, to the extent that their policies succeed, incumbent governments benefit when the process of economic adjustment is made smoother, thus avoiding painful layoffs, lower tax revenues, greater outlays of social benefits and the possibility of punishment at the polls. At the same time, other parts of the German economy must bear the costs of providing the public goods. In particular, the private, commercial banking industry in Germany, seeking a greater presence in both the domestic and international banking sectors, are placed at a significant competitive disadvantage. Thus, when the opportunity arose, the big commercial banks leapt at the chance to have the Landesbanken's financial privileges finally removed. But those who fiercely opposed changes to the status quo rallied to the defense of the bank and halted the Federal Government's compliance until the costs of refusal and the risk of losing out on future gains became apparent.

There is extensive social science and legal scholarship surrounding the *WestLB* case.[13] For example, Michael P. Smith (2001b) discusses how the case demonstrates the limited impact of EU liberalization pressures on the German model of capitalism. In contrast, Emiliano Grossman (2006) focuses on how the *WestLB* case assisted domestic political actors, and German commercial banks, to exit the political networks that inhibit policy change at the domestic level by generating a transnational alliance with the Commission through its prosecution of the German government for violating state aid rules.

Both authors address the implications European integration has had for German politics and its unique political economy. However, by putting the *WestLB* case in a different light, we can observe the politics of noncompliance. How and why did this case emerge? Why did the federal government delay its compliance? As much as the Court case shows how the winners, Germany's large commercial banks, benefitted from the enforcement of EU law, it also shows how the losers worked to create strong political allies that inhibited compliance. The regional banks, together with their Länder government allies, pulled the federal government away from complying until the other benefits related to European integration were put at risk.

The West LB case began in 1992, when the NRW government merged the *Wohnungsbauförderunganstalt des Landes NRW* (Wfa), a public housing company, with WestLB. The Land government was attempting to reduce the costs of administrating state public housing programs. The details of the transaction are important for explaining why the Commission eventually launched legal proceedings against the German government and the Landesbanken, and why they sought the removal of these banks' special guarantees as an illegal form of state aid. The NRW government had merged a nonprofit entity, Wfa, with a semi-public entity, WestLB, and increased the working capital available to the bank at an interest rate of 0.6 percent using its after-tax profits. Not only was the transfer carried out to reduce housing program costs, it was also necessary to meet Germany's obligations under the Own Funds Directive and Solvency

Ratio Directive.[14] The transfer of Wfa's assets to WestLB helped it to meet its legal reserve requirements without having to raise the capital on the open market, where it would have been much more expensive. While Wfa's capital assets remained in place to run housing programs, the assets were also made available to WestLB in order to increase its own funds such that they covered 5.6 percent of its risk-adjusted assets and risk-bearing off-balance-sheet transactions. Because WestLB was not forced to go to the open market to cover its risk exposure, the transfer of Wfa to WestLB amounted to a subsidy of €1 billion.

With their complaints unaddressed at the federal level, the *Bundesverband Deutscher Banken* (BdB) notified the Commission of the possible violation of EU state aid law by NRW and other Länder in 1994.[15] In 1997 the Commission finally opened a formal investigation under (now) Article 108(2). The Commission found in 1999 that proper remuneration to Wfa would be at the market rate of 9.3 percent. The Commission ordered the German government to reclaim 1.6 billion DM (or €82 million) with interest, which was the largest repayment of state aid in EU history. The Commission dismissed all of the *federal* government's arguments that the aid qualified as legitimate exemptions under Article 107, Sections (a–e).

WestLB did not accept the Commission's decision, however, and it sued the Commission. The case was brought before the European Court of Justice.[16] WestLB attempted to satisfy the Commission's demands by giving NRW a larger share in WestLB. The Commission did not find this solution satisfactory and launched a separate lawsuit against the German federal government for noncompliance with its decision.[17]

Neither the Member States nor the Commission anticipated such a strong policy regime to develop. When a EU competition policy was first emerging, most countries did not have a set of policies that either prohibited accumulated economic power among firms or state intervention in the economy. Most countries had some form of industrial policy. They use state funds to achieve regional or sector development or to rescue failing firms. The first elements of policy to deter government subsidies appeared in Articles 92–94 of the EC Treaty (now Article 107 TFEU). These provisions sought to prevent aid to national or subnational authorities from providing aid to companies that distorted competition. Numerous exceptions were included, such as aid to consumers, responses to natural disasters and, later, German financial assistance for the new Länder (Article 107(c) TFEU). The Council could also approve, by qualified majority voting, aid to promote development in regions with abnormally low levels of standard of living, high levels of unemployment, the development of specific economic activities, or to promote cultural or historic preservation (Articles 107(a–e)).

The first WestLB case raised further suspicions among Commission officials within DGIV about the larger benefits WestLB and other Landesbanken were enjoying as a result of state liability guarantees.[18] Although it appears the Commission was aware of and concerned about the state loan guarantees given to the Landesbanken as early as 1995, it did not start an investigation until it received second notification of a possible violation by the European Banking Federation (Grossman 2006: 337–338). The *Deutsche Sparkassen- und Giroverband* (DSGV), which represented all German public banks, and the *Bundesverband Öffentlicher Banken* (VÖB), which represents the Landesbanken, took the lead in fighting the Commission's decision. While they attempted to reach a compromise with the Commission, the latter body launched another formal investigation against the federal government on January 26, 2001. On July 17, 2001, all three parties reached an agreement whereby the state loan guarantees would end, but all loans already issued would still benefit from the guarantee until they expired, most in 2015 (Grossman 2006: 340–341).

Yet the Commission's supervision and monitoring of WestLB did not end in 2001. For example, when the NRW government removed the state guarantees in November 2001, it also injected capital of €2 billion into WestLB. The BdB complained once again to the Commission in 2002. In 2003 the BdB raised an additional complaint that NRW had violated EU state aid law by pursuing a silent participation with WestLB in the amount of €1.25 billion. The BdB also notified the Commission of additional capital injections that took place in 2005, totalling €471 million. But the Commission found these injections of capital as conforming to EU state aid rules.[19]

The survival of WestLB was put into doubt due to severe losses generated by the global financial crisis in 2008–09. The German federal government established a "bad bank" in order to relieve WestLB of over €85.1 billion in toxic and non-performing assets. The bank also received a capital injection of €3 billion. The European Commission gave temporary approval to the financial vehicle in 2009. However, strong suspicions about the amount of aid granted to WestLB were raised. The Commission started a formal investigation. It temporarily extended its authorization of German aid on June 22, 2010.[20] Ironically, in the original case that raised the Commission's suspicions of unlawful forms of state aid, the merger of Dfa and WestLB, the European Court of First Instance found in favor of WestLB, deciding that the Commission's arguments that WestLB was benefitting from an interest rate discount on the capital infusion from the merger were without foundation.[21]

The WestLB case does not just illustrate the ability of private commercial banks to use EU law to change the domestic status quo for their benefit. It also shows how a small number of actors worked hard to prevent the federal government from complying until the costs of not doing so became too exorbitant for the national government. But, when the stakes rose too high and jeopardized larger economic and political gains for Germany as a whole, the German government backed down.

As public banks for the Länder, they had easy access to strong political allies. According to Mitchell Smith, the directors of the Landesbanken emerge from the regional party leadership (Smith 2001b: 530). Even before formal proceedings against WestLB began, the Länder, led by Edmund Stoiber of Bavaria, led a council of state governments calling for the EU to refrain from intervening in state affairs.[22] The issue of the Landesbanken and their public nature resonated strongly with the growing opposition to European integration among Länder governments, irrespective of which party was in power. State governments were increasingly concerned about how the Commission and other EU institutions were delegated or were assuming more powers of governance, threatening Germany's brand of federalism and the sovereignty of the Länder.

But the ties between the Landesbanken and their regional government allies went beyond the defense of German federalism. The relationship appears to have been far more intimate. For example, in 1997 Johannes Rau of NRW, future German president, met with EU Commission President Jacques Santer and argued that the public banks were essential to the German system of banking (ibid.). Later, as German president, Rau faced accusations that he used a private plane during a re-election campaign in NRW provided by WestLB.[23] Leo Kirch, then-owner of Kirch Media and the "Rupert Murdoch" of Germany, had close connections to both the CSU and the Bavarian Landesbank, which was giving loans to support Kirch's failing businesses.[24] As the banks' legal relationships with state governments were being scrutinized, their questionable connections to other businessmen and methods of influencing politicians were also exposed.

Political allies also existed at the federal level. Chancellor Kohl attempted to secure protection for these state guarantees during negotiations over the Amsterdam Treaty in 1997, but ultimately failed. In addition, Horst Köhler, another future German president, was president of the savings bank association in the late 1990s, when the Commission's case against WestLB was first developing. He used his political clout as the former Vice Minister for Finance, and one of the leading negotiators over European monetary union, when defending the public banks before DG Competition Minister Karel van Miert (Grossman 2006: 339).

The private commercial banks in Germany had no equivalent political support. First, the Big Three simply did not have as large a presence in the German banking sector as the public banks. Second, as Grossman (2006) makes clear, the private banks always lacked significant political support from the federal government when they called for legislation to reduce the public banks' comparative advantage. When they did seek policies, private banks, such as Deutsche Bank, operated through the BdB out of fear of political backlash (Grossman 2006: 338). The only significant political support they received came from the Free Democratic Party (FDP) (Deeg 1999: 59, Smith 2001b: 531). The FDP saw common cause in the banks' efforts to generate greater market competition and reduce state involvement in the German economy. But, as the junior partner of the federal coalition and in the face of almost unanimous opposition by the Länder governments, it had little influence at the federal level (Smith 2001a: 133).

The dynamics of Germany's noncompliant behavior changed when the Länder governments threatened to stall European integration further. As the French European Council in 2000 started negotiations over institutional reform of the EU in light of future Eastern enlargement, European Affairs Minister Detlev Samland of NRW threatened to withhold the Länder's approval of these reforms unless the WestLB case was dropped or decided in their favor, gaining agreement from both Minister Presidents Stoiber of Bavaria and Henning Scherf of the state of Bremen.[25]

The heated rhetoric generated concern within the Kohl government that the WestLB case was beginning to threaten larger, more important foreign policy objectives. Germany was a strong supporter of Eastern enlargement and would not allow this dispute to delay it further (Schimmelfennig 2004). Some CDU leaders at the federal level, such as European Affairs spokesperson for the CDU/CSU party group, Peter Hintze, argued that the issues facing the Landesbanken were different from those related to the Sparkassen, which started to create a divide among the Länder governments over the proper solution to the WestLB case (Smith 2001b: 531). When the Commission ultimately issued its decision in 1999, the likelihood that WestLB would win its case was severely diminished. As Grossman argues, the case was beginning to strain relations between the federal government and the EU. "Nonetheless, the federal government appeared to be increasingly embarrassed and unwilling to defend the public banks' position with the same emphasis as the Länder did" (Grossman 2006: 341).

After the election of Gerhard Schröder as Chancellor in 2001, a compromise over the removal of the state guarantees was reached. Schröder did not just want to avoid strained relations with the Commission. The WestLB case was also a distraction from the government's larger efforts to make Frankfurt an international financial center that could rival both London and New York. The strategy, known as *Finanzplatz Deutschland*, started in the early 1980s and accelerated as European monetary union reached completion. The growing interest the German commercial banks had in securities markets and the issuing of equities made the competition between the commercial banks and the Landesbanken over loans to small and medium-sized enterprises in Germany less relevant (Deeg 1999: 87–95).[26] But the domestic commercial banks also did not want the Landesbanken to use their state loan guarantees to obtain greater and cheaper amounts of capital for investment banking compared to the rates they faced as they both attempted to expand their global investment activities.

Coupled with greater liberalization of financial services at the EU level and a political ideology far more friendly to the free market, namely the SPD's party program of a "*Neue Mitte*," the possibility that the German federal government would defend the public banks' loan guarantee looked increasingly remote. Thus, even though WestLB eventually won its case before the Court of First Instance, its influence was waning. The shrill nature of the debate and its increasing irrelevancy as investment banking became more dominant led the federal government eventually to engineer a compromise between WestLB and the other Landesbanken, the Länder governments and the Commission.

This short case study puts the WestLB case in a new perspective that allows us to observe the process and politics of noncompliance. First, the German government did not ever foresee that its system of providing informal loan guarantees to regional development banks would challenge state aid rules. The case of the German banks only emerged as the Commission was pursuing litigation against other banks in Italy (Grossman 2006: 336).

Second, the German government was pulled away from compliance more than it was pushed towards it. German commercial banks were able to exercise an "exit option" and cooperate with the Commission to undo the status quo, which speaks to much of the IR literature on compliance (Dai 2005, Simmons 2009). However, the commercial banks, as the winners associated with compliance, were not as willing or able to push the federal government to comply as the losers prevented it. First, as Grossman shows, the commercial banks became increasingly reluctant to challenge the federal government because of mounting losses from many lost legislative battles. Also, compared to the Landesbanken, their gains were large and diffuse. The removal of the Länders' loan guarantees would place them on an equally competitive footing with not only the Big Three German banks, but foreign banks as well.

In contrast, the losses for the Landesbanken were highly concentrated. They stood to lose an important comparative advantage in providing banking services to small and medium-sized enterprises as international economic competition grew. These loan guarantees also enabled these banks to pursue investment strategies at far less risk than their commercial peers. Therefore, they capitalized on their connections to state governments to withhold compliance. The significant role these banks played in the German economy also enabled them to garner widespread support for their case across party lines.

Over time, however, the federal government, which was the defendant in the case, did not want to sacrifice the substantial long-term gains of EU expansion in order to satisfy the regional banks and their government sponsors. In addition, widespread support for WestLB did not emerge among the general public. First, the average German cared very little about the battles between the richest segments of German society. Second, the financial sector in Germany was divided over the Landesbanken's special capital provisions. Third, growing threats by Länder governments to stall EU expansion placed a key foreign policy of the federal government at risk. As a result, both the Kohl and Schröder governments pushed for a deal to solve the case before it reached the ECJ.

It is too soon to claim that the German banking system has been significantly liberalized or transformed as a result of EU legal pressures (Deeg 1999, Schmidt 2002). The EU's tolerance so far of state intervention to save struggling German banks in the wake of the recent financial crisis shows the EU is not determined to see the German financial industry entirely liberalized. And the German government will always seek to protect these banks and other patterns of state intervention, such as development assistance to the new, eastern Länder, at the negotiating table. The institutional patterns and networks that sustain long-term investment in German SMEs are too strong to be removed by a small number of Court cases. But, the goal here is not to assess how much Europeanization or globalization is transforming Germany's financial system or consensus-based economic model. Instead, the case study suggests where we can find the greatest opposition to these forces, how they mobilize to prevent change, and ultimately why they win or lose.

Rescuing Rover in Britain

The Landesbanken had a strong and important presence in the German economy and political system. The state loan guarantees gave them a strong competitive edge over their rivals. The Rover case, in contrast, deals with a firm that was in severe decline in a rapidly declining industry. By the late 1970s, MG Rover was the last major automobile manufacturer that existed in the United Kingdom. And unless it secured financial assistance from the British government, it faced certain death. The British government's decision to come to the rescue is somewhat paradoxical. A neoliberal, anti-statist government that viewed state ownership and subsidies as an anathema provided the necessary financial assistance to help MG Rover merge with British Aerospace (BAe). The Commission discovered this state assistance when it became public in the form of a Parliamentary investigation. It determined the state aid was illegal and forced the British government to retrieve these funds. Despite being one of the most euroskeptic governments in British and European history, the Thatcher government eventually complied with the Commission's demands, before the ECJ even ruled on the matter.

Finding a case of state aid and even noncompliance with EU law in the United Kingdom is an unusual expectation. First, as is widely acknowledged in the comparative political economy literature, the UK is an exemplar of "market-based" capitalism. In contrast to Germany, close ties between banks, both of a public and a commercial nature, and firms are absent. British firms generally receive most of their capital on the open market from private investment banks. Rather than pursuing long-term investment strategies, British firms concentrate on the short term. As we will see, MG Rover exemplifies this pattern.

Britain's production profile is also markedly different from Germany's. Because of an over-valued pound sterling, the commitment of maintaining preferential trading relationships with the Commonwealth countries, and a relatively less skilled workforce, British manufacturers focused on low-quality, mass-produced goods. Based on a *laissez-faire* doctrine, the British government allowed the market to push workers from manufacturing into the growing service sector of the economy. During this period of economic decline in the 1970s through the early 1990s, the British government remained on the sidelines. In general, the British model of capitalism relied on Keynesian and then monetarist forms of macroeconomic management to guide the process of economic adjustment.

Although the British model of capitalism is best described as one with little coordination between the state and business, this does not imply that the state stood idly by as the competitiveness of British manufacturing declined. State financial assistance did flow to specific firms on an *ad hoc* basis. Informal networks of leading British businessmen and ministerial officials led to state investment in firms, mainly in emergency situations (Grant and Sargent 1987).

The Department of Trade and Industry (DTI) in the 1970s and early 1980s epitomized this practice.[27] The close personal and political connections between ministry officials and leading business executives led to state assistance, which often raised suspicions of corruption. The programs the government devised also generally lacked specific details as to how to engineer turnarounds. During the Thatcher years, the anathema towards state subsidies for industry only grew stronger. The Thatcher government pursued a concerted policy of deregulation, liberalization and privatization. Labor protections and the power of unions were reduced. Vivien Schmidt also argues that the intimate relationship between civil servants and managers began to fade (Schmidt 2002: 161). Instead, independent regulatory agencies proliferated, seeking to enforce market rules rather than intervene in specific circumstances.

Finding noncompliance in the UK is also unexpected, given Margaret Thatcher's view of British interests in regard to European integration. Her support for European integration mainly flowed from her desire to see trade barriers fall across the Continent. She was also strongly skeptical of the significant amounts of financial aid that flowed from Brussels to declining industries or poor regions in the rest of the EU, leading her to demand the British rebate. Thatcher perceived European integration as an opportunity to pursue her neoliberal ideology on the Continent and perhaps strengthen the UK's economic presence, particularly in the financial sector, as a result.

Yet, Thatcher and the Conservative Party at the time were also highly skeptical of EU authority. She and her party did not perceive more power delegated to Brussels as necessary to fulfill her vision of the EU's purpose. Rather than reregulation in Brussels, she saw the removal of trade barriers and discriminatory regulatory practices as the Commission's chief tasks. She and her party also viewed with great concern the loss of British national sovereignty. The growing role of the ECJ, its ability to overrule Parliamentary law, and the Commission's powers to investigate and control national policies, all generated great opposition in the Thatcher government at the time. The role of the EU in Britain generated serious divisions within the Conservative party with Thatcher's opponents and supporters coming to be known as the "wets" and the "drys" respectively.

Thus, the UK's positions on the EU and its policies look increasingly Janus-faced. On the one hand, it strongly supported the agenda and purpose of European integration, which was purportedly the deregulation of national economies. On the other hand, the Conservative government, which ruled Britain from 1981 to 1997, opposed the growing role EU law played within Britain's policy-making and legal system. Therefore, we would expect the British government's strong opposition to EU supranational authority should lead it to refuse to comply with EU institutions when it becomes an issue. Thus, if the ECJ issued a ruling against the UK for violating EU law, we would expect continued strategies to avoid compliance. The British government might also appeal to its co-Member States in the EU Council and seek legislation that would reverse the ECJ's or Commission's decision. While unlikely to emerge victorious, the British government's strong reluctance to accept EU authority over significant political matters would at least lead it to seek legislation that would allow it to sustain the status quo.

In the Rover case we find none of these outcomes. First, despite the Thatcher government's aversion to state subsidies of firms and industries, and the watchful eye of the Commission, the British government gave unlawful aid to the Rover group in order both to pursue its policy of privatization and to save the last automobile factory in Britain. Saving Rover, however, would come at the expense of the rest of British society and what proved to be a waste of state resources. Rover's close political connections to DTI enabled it to receive state assistance unbeknownst to Members of Parliament.

Despite the Government's efforts to save Rover, national political support to save it from the Commission's efforts to enforce state aid law never materialized. First, the government hid some of the key aspects of the state aid that was awarded. Second, despite job losses in a region of Britain experiencing significant economic decline, Labour sided with the Commission in criticizing the government's deal with BAe. Once the EU's investigation began, the Commission asked BAe to return a significant portion of the state aid it had received. However, the ECJ intervened and ruled against the Commission's decision seeking repayment. Despite Britain's legal victory, the government still complied given the long-term, larger gains European integration would produce. Thus, even in an unlikely case as the UK under Thatcher, the Rover case follows closely my model of noncompliance.

The decline of Britain's last major car producer began in the 1970s. The Rover Group emerged as a result of a series of mergers sponsored by the government in order for the industry to compete more effectively with its American and Japanese competitors. The British Leyland Motor Corporation collapsed financially in 1973. The government then nationalized it in 1974, made it part of the National Enterprise Board and renamed it BL. The group manufactured models of the Range Rover, Jaguar, Austin and Mini brands.[28] Even though the Government invested more than £900 million total in the 1970s, the company continued to lose money and market share. The Thatcher government decided to privatize the group in 1986, then renaming it once more the Rover Group.

The Rover Group suffered from chronic issues of overcapacity and a lack of international competitiveness. Massive shifts in manufacturing methods and technology began to make the cars Rover made highly obsolete. The development of just-in-time or flexible production in Japan, as well as large, multinational car companies in the US, namely Ford and General Motors, put Rover at a huge competitive disadvantage. Rover had neither a highly skilled workforce nor large economies of scale. Thus, it could not compete either in the high-end, specialized automobile sector or among low-end mass-produced cars. There was also a chronic lack of any concentrated and coordinated investment in the company's workers, product line or production technologies. In 1979, the new managing director, Michael Edwardes, reformed labor relations through confrontation with the union and lowered wages (Berkeley *et al.* 2005). But an overvalued pound and absence of any nationally coordinated policy of investment only accelerated the decline of the sole remaining domestic automobile manufacturer in the United Kingdom. Rover was a prime candidate for receiving bailout funds from the government.

The arrival of the Thatcher government led to concerted efforts to reduce British state intervention in the economy. In 1980 the British government was BL's banker, major shareholder and strongest political benefactor (McLaughlin and Maloney 1996). A BL board supervised the company, which consisted of the Chief Ministers from DTI, Treasury, Employment and an official from 10 Downing Street Policy Unit. As losses began to mount in the early 1980s, the Thatcher government decided to accelerate plans to privatize the company. But fierce infighting between the members of the board led to failures to sell off the company. Edwardes' refusal to reorganize the company along 10 Downing Street wishes stalled a partnership with Honda, which would have brought much needed Japanese technology and production knowledge to BL. There were also reported differences between DTI, led by Sir Leon Brittan, and 10 Downing Street, which complicated the sale of BL to both Ford and GM. In both cases, 10 Downing Street wanted to sell off the full assets of BL to either Ford or GM, but DTI and Conservative backbenchers in Parliament refused to see the last British car company under foreign ownership (ibid.: 442–445).[29] Thus, there was some nationalist sentiment generated to support saving Rover.

But, after the election of 1987, the pressure to privatize Rover only grew within the Government. Although a long-term partnership with Honda that presented itself made more business sense, the government was seeking a short-term solution. In November 1987 the Chairman of BAe, Professor Roland Smith, approached the government and expressed his interest in purchasing Rover. The deal would satisfy everyone politically. The government could proceed quickly with the privatization. In addition, many believed the merger would generate new synergies. BAe's chairman saw a chance to combine the technology generated by its defense sector with manufacturing high-end cars, such as Land Rover, pursuing the same strategy as Saab-Scania in Sweden. Finally, the sale of Rover to BAe would keep Rover in the hands of a British company, pleasing the more nationalistic Conservative backbenchers.

The British government disregarded Ford's right to claim Rover's assets first and offered a generous deal to BAe instead. In addition to certain tax breaks and the sale of all government shares in Rover for £150 million, the British government would inject more than £800 million to eliminate Rover's indebtedness. In turn, BAe agreed not to sell off the Austin and Land Rover brands for five years. Security analysts from the City of London viewed it as the "deal of the century."[30] Or, in the view of Lord Young, then head of DTI, it was "the deal of the decade" for the British taxpayer, which immediately raised the suspicions of the Commission.

The European Commission had initiated a strong initiative in the 1980s to rationalize the car industries among the Member States and reduce state involvement in the automobile sector. DGIV and others were actively seeking to remove state subsidies and other forms of financial assistance that Member States gave their national car industries. In March 1988 the British government notified the Commission it was selling Rover to BAe. The Commission immediately viewed the cash injection and reduction in Rover's debt burden with suspicion. It initiated an investigation under Article 108(2).

Correspondence between the Competition Directorate and the British government continued through 1988. In July of 1988 the Commission issued its decision that the sale amount was illegal under Article 107.[31] In the past, the Commission approved almost all injections of state funds into BL between 1975 and 1987, which, according to the Commission, amounted to almost £3 billion in equity capital, even though BL had not had a financially profitable year since 1976. Prime Minister Thatcher desperately wanted to end these practices. In June 1988, before Commissioner Sutherland issued his ruling on the sale, Thatcher sent a letter to Commission President Jacques Delors to intervene and approve the deal.[32] Despite these appeals, the Commission ruled that the British government underestimated the total debt the Rover Group held and calculated that BAe was actually being paid to take over Rover. Thus, under EU state aid rules, the deal could go through only if the government reduced its offer to £469 million, such that BAe would still hold £100 million in Rover debt. The Commission also canceled a £231 million tax write-off for BAe.

Lord Young's efforts to prevent a Commission investigation had failed. Meanwhile, opposition to the deal was also growing at home. Labour MPs Tony Blair and Gordon Brown began questioning why BAe was being given such a generous offer. In addition, other foreign firms from Europe, such as VW and Ford, were looking to purchase Rover if the deal with BAe fell through. It was also highly unlikely that DGIV would back down. It had just conditionally approved French government aid to Renault in the form of debt relief and capital injections, over Sutherland's objections, and was starting to investigate the "artificially low price" of the sale of Alfa-Romeo to Fiat. If the Commission had allowed the sale of Rover to BAe to go forward on the British government's original terms, it would have lost credibility with other Member State governments in other investigations. In turn, they would also call for the removal of the conditions the Commission had imposed on them in their transactions with automobile companies, leading to a ratcheting up, rather than reduction, in state intervention in the automobile industry.

Still, Chairman Smith of BAe bemoaned what he perceived as illegitimate interference in national affairs and thought the new price for assuming Rover's debts was far too high. He issued a statement suggesting BAe was going to walk away from the deal.[33] Interestingly, Lord Young saved the arrangement with only 24 hours remaining. On July 14 Lord Young told a pleasantly surprised House of Commons, "Nothing has changed between yesterday and today. The only change is that BAe has clarified the position over terms satisfactory to them." Unbeknownst to Parliament at the time, the deal had changed significantly.

On November 29, 1988 someone leaked documents to *The Guardian* newspaper that the sale of Rover to BAe contained secret "sweeteners." In a confidential memorandum to BAe, Members of Parliament, the National Audit Office and DTI, Lord Young promised an additional £38 million in financial assistance not previously disclosed to Parliament or the Commission.[34] The letter to BAe chairman listed three payments in ascending order according to the risk that they would raise the suspicions of the Commission as being unlawful forms of state aid. The memo to BAe demonstrates the powerful and authoritative role the Commission's competition policy was playing, even in the UK. The legal regime surrounding the awarding of state aid is so rigorous that the head of DTI chose to use secret methods to avoid its scrutiny.

The details of the deal were not made public until the National Audit Office issued an official report seventeen months after the deal was concluded. Strongly committed to avoiding a foreign takeover of Rover, Lord Young hid the deal from lawmakers by placing the details of the trade among numerous obscure parliamentary documents marked confidential.[35] Concerns were also raised that the Government had undervalued the deal by £56 million.

The disclosure of the sweeteners unleashed outrage among Members of Parliament. Although Parliament was controlled by the incumbent Conservative Party, there were numerous investigations across different parliamentary committees that included all political parties. Conservative Party members' anger at the deal focused on the total price of privatizing Rover, increasing the burden borne by the British taxpayer. Labour MPs criticized the deal for taking place behind closed doors and keeping Parliament uninformed. Lord Young defended the deal in the House of Lords by arguing he was trying to save 40,000 jobs at Rover and 50,000 more among Rover's suppliers and distributors.[36] Nicholas Ridley, the new State Secretary for Trade and Industry, defended the additional payments as not qualifying as state aid. Neil Kinnock, then-Labour Party leader, criticized Thatcher for wasting taxpayers' money as well as hiding the deal from the public, stating, "Methinks the lady doth protest too much. Will you tell us now, did you or did you not know on Tuesday that the sale had been sweetened with £38 million of taxpayers' money in handouts?"[37] Prime Minister Thatcher argued that it was the best deal the Government could obtain and also denied misleading Parliament.

Most importantly, the disclosure of the deal threatened Britain's long-term interests in European integration. First, as Labour MPs argued, Thatcher could no longer criticize other nations for unlawfully subsidizing their automobile industries. The Prime Minister would lose all her credibility in criticizing state intervention in the economy by other Member State governments. Second, deception of the Commission threatened the UK's decision to join the European Rate Mechanism by reducing the Government's credibility. Labour MP Gordon Brown stated, "How can the Prime Minister tell other countries in good faith that they should abolish hidden subsidies before she joins the European monetary system, when a hidden subsidy is exactly what the Prime Minister has allowed to happen?"[38] Even a Labour MP representing the Coventry district, where most of the jobs would be lost if the deal had not gone through, accused the Government of incompetence and corruption. Furthermore, additional accusations of corruption were raised when MPs noted that Norman Tebbit, another former DTI minister, moved from there to serve as chief advisor to BAe's executive board. Finally, despite the sale of Rover to BAe, more than 4,900 jobs were eliminated at the Cowley South and Llanelli car plants to reduce overcapacity.

In light of these reports, the Commission initiated an investigation in 1990 and issued a decision that BAe was required to repay the British government £44.4 million for violating Article 1 of its previous decision on the Rover sale. Announced by Sir Leon Brittan, who had been appointed EC Competition Commissioner, this was the largest financial penalty the Commission had ever imposed on a British company. It appears the decision was delayed in Brussels due to suspicion that Brittan was being too lenient on his native country.[39] At the same time, Brittan was attempting to maintain his Directorate's credibility in light of his recent order that the French government retrieve more than FFr12 billion from Renault. If Britain was not punished, President Delors might also have requested the Directorate to drop its demands of repayment against France. The Commission then launched Article 108(2) proceedings against the British government, demanding it retrieve the unlawful funds that had also been hidden from the EC.[40]

Despite the growing domestic and EU pressures for repayment, BAe and Rover challenged the Commission's decision before the ECJ in 1992. In their suit, lodged under Article 230, BAe argued that the Commission had breached Article 108(2) of the EC Treaty by not following proper legal procedures. The ECJ agreed and annulled the Commission's decision that required repayment of £44.4 million. Despite losing the case before the Court, Sir Leon vowed to continue the investigation.

BAe's victory before the ECJ gave some momentum to its view on whether it would have to pay back the state aid it received. But both Sir Leon and BAe knew it was a pyrrhic victory. The Court did not address the substance of the Commission's claims that the assistance was illegal under EU state aid rules. The Competition Directorate would immediately relaunch its case against BAe and the British government. Fearing a protracted legal battle, BAe decided to return the money. In response, BAe repaid the British government over £57.6 million, the original £44.4 million and £13.2 million in interest. The case of noncompliance against the British government was terminated.

In spite of all of these efforts, BAe began to suffer its own financial difficulties and subsequently sold the Rover Group off to BMW, in a highly controversial deal. The lack of investment in Rover by BMW, as well as difficulties associated with different management cultures, led them to sell Rover in turn to the British Phoenix Consortium for £10, which renamed it the MG Rover Group. The Consortium still could not turn the firm around, mostly due to the overvalued pound and a lack of additional state assistance from the British government.

In 2005 MG Rover went into receivership. More than 6,500 workers were laid off and the Longbridge plant in Birmingham, England, formerly the largest manufacturing plant in the world and original home of the Austin Mini, was shut. The Chinese automobile company Nanjing Motors purchased the remaining assets and now employs 200 workers at the plant to produce the MG TF. The Government purchased the rest of the Longbridge factory's land for redevelopment into housing and industry. In the end, all of the Government's efforts to save Rover and keep it in British hands, which cost billions of pounds and tested

British compliance with EU law, proved completely ineffective and all for naught in preventing the death of Rover.

The case of the Rover Group reveals many of the same dynamics that cause noncompliance elsewhere in the European Union. First, the British government did not anticipate the Commission developing an aggressive competition policy as well as a strong supranational authority. Upon joining the EC, Britain's primary goal was to seek greater access for its exports and to ensure London's place in global and European financial markets. At the same time, Britain's primary concern was to safeguard its trading privileges with the Commonwealth countries, limit the costs of the CAP and prevent any drift away from the US among its European allies (Moravcsik 1998). Over time, subsidies to poorer regions and industries also generated greater concern, leading Thatcher to demand the British rebate. However, British farmers and, later, the regions experiencing massive deindustrialization, such as the West Midlands where Rover was located, received considerable EU financial assistance. Saving British manufacturing was partly the purpose behind European integration. Since 1973 British governments repeatedly underestimated the costs of doing so, even if it was a top priority to join the European Community at the time.

Second, as in many other EU Member States, the UK's skepticism of a federal Europe did not prevent the development of a rigorous competition policy at the EU level. The Competition Directorate became one of the most powerful elements of the EU bureaucracy. It could operate independently of the Member States and affect their core national interests. Unlike other compliance procedures, the Competition Directorate required governments to obtain approval from it first before awarding financial assistance to troubled firms or industries. It could also bypass some of the other procedures in Article 258 and go directly to the ECJ if a country refused to comply. Of course, this was in every Member State's interest. In the sensitive world of state aid, every government has a strong incentive to free ride in order to maintain the status quo to the benefit of powerful political allies or to avert massive layoffs. And no state has an incentive to monitor another. In addition, the removal of market distortions, deregulation, privatization, and reducing state intervention in the economy were key objectives of the Thatcher government. Thus, despite the Conservative party's growing opposition to the EU authority, Britain's national interests and the EU's enforcement of state aid rules generally aligned with each other.

As a result, the Rover case is an interesting paradox. First, in order to privatize Rover, the government was well aware it needed to offer generous financial incentives to any possible buyer. In the entire history of state ownership of Rover, and despite over £3 billion spent on keeping Rover afloat, there was never a coherent investment strategy or program to make it profitable over the long term. The government would rely on *ad hoc* partnerships struck with Honda, capital infusions from the sale of Jaguar, and possible mergers with Ford or GM in order to save Rover. There were no efforts to devalue sterling, develop long-term access to capital or train new workers to compete more effectively with European, Japanese and American competitors, illustrative of Britain's political economy.

Second, the deal to save Rover itself also reflects the nature of government–business ties in the UK. BAe was the preferred buyer because of its close connections to the government. Also, the sale to BAe would satisfy latent nationalist sentiments among Conservative Party members. Most importantly, given the cost of the deal, only Rover, BAe and perhaps some workers in the West Midlands would benefit from the deal, although evidence that the deal would save jobs at Rover is hard to find. While the benefits were concentrated, the losses would be borne by the British taxpayer and diffused across the population, although significant in aggregate. Although the costs for each individual British taxpayer were low, the revelation of these "sweeteners" through scandal magnified these costs in the eyes of both the public and the Labour Party. Therefore, it is no surprise that the deal did not generate widespread support by the general public. This fact partly explains why the British government and BAe complied with the Commission's demands, despite there being no legal judgment against them.

Apart from the government and BAe, no one else had a vested interest in saving Rover. Although it was the last of Britain's car manufacturing plants, saving it could not generate widespread public support. In the atmosphere of British economic decline and high unemployment, the demise of Rover represented just another failure of British industry. It came at the end of British industrial decline, not at the beginning, when there would have been some more hope of saving it. In addition, the government did not bother to rally bipartisan support. By keeping the deal hidden from the Commission and the House of Commons, the government did not just anger the public and MPs. Labour also withdrew any support of the deal. The Labour Party believed the scandal over Rover was an opportunity to embarrass Thatcher, and even bring down her government. Thus, in marked contrast to each of the other cases of noncompliance considered in this book, the Rover case showed how broad support for maintaining the status quo is necessary to sustain a case of noncompliance to an ECJ ruling.

The government also acknowledged that continued noncompliance put longer-term policy objectives at risk. These included Britain's decision to join the ERM and the completion of the single market. Discussions over the enlargement of the European Union also began with the end of the Cold War. The UK could not afford to sacrifice its interests in future European integration on the altar of Rover. Therefore, in spite of being one of the most euroskeptic governments in British history and contemptuous of EU authority, the British government retrieved its aid from BAe and complied with EU state aid law.

Conclusion

This chapter has compared cases of noncompliance in two countries where noncompliance is least likely to occur. First, the state aid regime is one of the most legalized policy areas in the European Union. It has strong mechanisms to monitor noncompliance by forcing states to notify the Commission if state aid is given. There is a rigorous legal process by which to prosecute and punish states for awarding illegitimate forms of state aid. Second, although the precise rules and regulations governing states were left unclear and vague for almost thirty years after the EC Treaty was signed, litigation and rulemaking at the Council level in the 1980s began to clarify the Member States' legal obligations. Therefore, the causes of compliance that both the management and enforcement schools put forward were addressed over time within the state aid legal regime.

As a result, compliance with state aid rules is very high compared to other policy areas as well as to other legal instruments the EU uses to foster European economic integration. Notification of state aid to DGIV is high. The number of negative decisions issued by the Commission, to the extent we can measure them, is quite low. In addition, levels of state aid over time have decreased over time (Blauberger 2009), which was one of the Commission's chief goals. Aid targeted for specific industries is also lower than in the past.

Yet, despite the elements for good compliance being present, we still observe noncompliance happening. And it varies across the Member States. First, unsurprisingly, noncompliance is a function of how governments subsidize their industries. Therefore, whether states have historical policy traditions of intervening in the national economy probably plays a strong role in determining why cases of noncompliance occur. Yet, this only means the probability of noncompliance occurring is higher in these countries, not necessarily what its causes are. By examining cases of noncompliance in countries without a tradition of state support for industry, we can better understand why noncompliance happens and why some cases are settled sooner than others.

In Chapter 3 I studied why some cases were referred to the European Court of Justice in two countries that strongly support European integration. This chapter looks at noncompliance also in unlikely situations, but in terms of whether governments award significant amounts of state aid. Neither the UK nor Germany provide generous amounts of state aid, with some exceptions, such as Germany's continued financial assistance to the new Länder. Noncompliance happens because the losses of removing state aid from specific firms are concentrated. The benefits of complying are distributed across the national population. The losers also have informational advantages. As both the WestLB and Rover cases show, the firms affected by the removal of their state assistance used their political connections to fight for maintaining the status quo.

However, neither country delayed noncompliance until the ECJ issued its ruling. In neither case did widespread support by the general public emerge to delay noncompliance In the Rover case, the scandalous nature associated with awarding the aid prevented cross-party cooperation in defending aid to Rover, in spite of the effect it would have on an already beleaguered part of the country. In Germany, more widespread support for maintaining the German Landesbanken system emerged among the Länder leadership. Because these banks helped the Länder finance important development and restructuring policies, they had strong allies against the Commission's demand. However, like Britain, German society was divided over maintaining their special privileges. First, the German private banks, namely Deutsche Bank, worked hard to mobilize support for compliance. Second, the general public was ignorant or unconcerned about the effect compliance would have on national society, especially compared to changing the Beer Purity law. Repeated reports of corruption and personal ties between the Landesbanken representatives and Länder governments did not strengthen public support for delayed compliance.

The national governments in both countries did attempt to protect their respective losers by changing the laws themselves. Chancellor Kohl sought legal protection for the public banks during negotiations over the Amsterdam Treaty. Prime Minister Thatcher attempted to influence President Jacques Delors to overrule Commissioner Brittan's decision. Both failed to generate any EU-wide support. Support for both Britain and Germany would bring additional attention to the policies that other Member States provided to their industries. For example, the Commission only began investigating the German public banks while pursuing a similar case against Italian government support for its banks.

Finally, despite the national sensitivity of the Rover and WestLB cases, both governments complied before the ECJ issued final rulings on the matter, even when they achieved pyrrhic victories before the Court of Justice. Continued disputes between the Landesbanken, the Länder and the Commission were jeopardizing negotiations over EU enlargement. The federal government did not want to forestall Eastward expansion, a key foreign policy goal that was assumed to benefit all Germans, in order to protect the public banks. In comparison, Thatcher was firmly committed to privatizing the Rover Group. But the discovery of the shady deal between DTI and BAe threatened Britain's credibility as it sought membership in the ERM. Even though Thatcher was a fierce opponent of Brussels power and was challenging a core policy initiative, eventually Rover repaid the aid. Thus, the general model of noncompliance offered here explains why noncompliance occurred even in these unsuspecting cases and why these countries only delayed complying instead of acting very reluctantly.

5 Conclusion

Summary of the argument

In general, we know much about why states comply with international law. They comply because it is either in their interest to do so or because of the law's normative pull. This assumes that the international treaties or other components of international law, such as customary international law, require significant changes to the national status quo. But we know comparatively less about why states don't comply. If this is the case, governments must play a "two-level" game and balance their international legal obligations against sometimes-powerful domestic interests that oppose compliance.

Compliance with international law can be considered a public good for a country. When states decide to conclude international agreements, they are making efforts to improve upon the status quo. However, when the good is public and the gains produced from cooperation are nonrival and nonexcludable, there are strong incentives to free ride. Unless states can obtain the gains only through participation, or other members notice it, governments will rationally choose to free ride. As a result, international agreements often contain enforcement provisions, management mechanisms to assist cooperation, and extensive legal procedures to adjudicate disputes. In fact, this study confirms the findings of others (Zürn and Neyer 2005) that high levels of legalization lead to better rates of compliance. This proves true whether one is comparing different international regimes or even within the same international regime.

Despite these efforts to secure compliance, noncompliance still happens. There are four types of (non)compliance behavior. First, states might comply immediately and continuously over time. Either the benefits outweigh the costs or the threats of punishment are credible and/or of a sufficient magnitude. States comply immediately also because this constitutes appropriate behavior for a modern, democratic state. Yet, problems of noncompliance can emerge because of exogenous shocks, because the losers created by a new international agreement were not sufficiently compensated, or because of the uncertainty and unintended consequences of a newly created international rule. These losses are usually concentrated among a small group of firms or individuals, who are then more likely to mobilize against compliance than the general population or even the winners. They also have informational advantages over others. Because international institutions are more likely to use their powers to enforce international law against noncompliant actors rather than reward winners, the losers have a *de facto* informational advantage over the beneficiaries associated with compliance.

The losers generated by compliance are, therefore, more likely to mobilize to protect the status quo than winners will organize to change it. Groups affected by compliance use special access to sympathetic lawmakers to lobby governments to delay the legislation required for compliance. A state can also refuse to implement the necessary legislation to comply completely with its legal obligations, leading to repeated investigations and complaints by international institutions, as was shown in the case of the German Beer Purity law. Government politicians respond to this pressure by not immediately complying, either because they have important constituencies or because these groups obtain broader public support. The targeted state practices may also be central to the government's policy agenda. For example, both the granting of loan guarantees to the German Landesbanken and subsidies to BAe to purchase Rover were key components of government policies and practices.

Yet, when there are high levels of legalization, national governments will eventually choose to comply. Legalization allows states to justify their practices before a court of law. Governments can then present arguments to the court for why the status quo should be allowed to continue. In addition, the costs are relatively low for the entire country, albeit concentrated among a few politically powerful actors. Once the ECJ makes its ruling, Member State governments are reluctant to sacrifice the gains of current or future cooperation. EU and national politics win out over domestic opposition to compliance.

In a few cases, governments win by persuading both the Commission and the ECJ that the existing status quo does not violate EU law, as the French did in *Cinématique*. However, governments lose more than three-quarters of the cases that are brought before the ECJ judges. Thus, governments use ECJ rulings that are against them to justify policy changes that domestic audiences otherwise would oppose vociferously. In addition, the Rover and Landesbanken cases show how important upcoming negotiations over further steps in cooperation at the European level can serve as an impetus for national governments to solve problems of noncompliance before they jeopardize ongoing negotiations and future possible gains.

Even in the EU, however, complete noncompliance, or refusal, still occurs. Not all compliance regimes in the EU are created equal. Unlike the legal regimes that focus on the free movement of goods and state aid, the compliance mechanisms under European Monetary Union (EMU) are comparatively weak. While strong enforcement mechanisms are listed in the agreement, they lack any credibility. The conditions for compliance are quite vague. There are also few policies in place to assist countries when they attempting to meet the eurozone's economic and fiscal criteria for membership. In fact, they are explicitly excluded and prohibited. Finally, the regime surrounding the Maastricht criteria is not fully legalized. There is no independent, neutral arbiter that can adjudicate legal disputes over compliance with the criteria.

At the domestic level, the costs of complying are not just significant, but are borne by large segments of the population. There are also few linkages between membership in the monetary union and steps towards additional European cooperation in other areas, such as fiscal policy. As a result, there is extensive free riding and noncompliance. This pattern of behavior became fully exposed during the recent Greek financial crisis, as well as during the short history of the euro. The failure of states to comply with the Maastricht criteria shows that the causes of noncompliance are similar to other cases. But, in contrast to the case studies already presented, eurozone members refused to change the status quo. Only a crisis that threatened the future of the euro itself pushed the Member States into making significant changes to the status quo. Even then, governments decided not to implement the necessary mechanisms to prevent future noncompliance and another possible crisis.

Noncompliance with the Maastricht criteria

The history of European monetary integration is well known.[1] EU Member States were interested in monetary integration in order to combat the exchange rate instability that ensued after the United States unilaterally abandoned the gold standard. Western European countries then attempted various exchange-rate arrangements to restore stability. Monetary cooperation and integration began with the creation of the European Rate Mechanism, or "Snake," in 1971 under the Smithsonian Agreement. Most EEC countries pegged their currencies to the value of a floating dollar. In 1972 the "Snake in the Tunnel" was put into place to allow greater flexibility to adjust to international financial pressures.

In the wake of hyperinflation and balance of payments crises, the Snake ended in 1974 when France left the system and the remaining currencies became an effective DM zone, which included Denmark and the Benelux countries, Germany's main trading partners. In 1979 European cooperation resumed as macroeconomic performance and policies among the weak-currency countries converged around commitments to fiscal policy austerity. As in the early 1970s, Germany became concerned again about the appreciation of the Deutsche mark. The European Monetary System and the European Rate Mechanism were established as a result. These were successful in maintaining currency stability in Europe. Combined with the completion of the single European market and good economic growth in the 1980s, the conditions were favorable for increased European monetary integration.

In 1991, at Maastricht, EU Member States finally agreed to create a single European currency and the rules for its operation and membership. One school of thought attributes Germany's and France's decision to solidify plans for European Monetary Union as a function of "high politics." The French government insisted that Germany sacrifice the power of the Deutsche mark on the altar of Europe as the price for German reunification, and the then-Chancellor Helmut Kohl willingly agreed (Baun 1995, 1996). Another school of thought argues that the agreement reached at Maastricht reflects the convergence of national interests and intergovernmental bargaining on the basis of those interests (Moravcsik 1998).

We need not rehearse the entire history of EMU negotiations here. Nor do I weigh the relative explanatory power of competing theories. Instead, my focus is on how the bargaining outcome actually contained the seeds of future noncompliance, despite the intense efforts of German negotiators throughout the process. First, none of the necessary features for a successful compliance regime were put into place to prevent noncompliance. Tools from any of the three schools of compliance – enforcement, management or legalization – were missing. In addition, the three main sources of noncompliance – uncompensated losers, vague legal language and unanticipated consequences – were also present. Also, in contrast to earlier cases of noncompliance, the costs of complying were high and distributed across the national population. Many domestic actors had enormous influence on national governments that blocked changes to the status quo. As a result, total noncompliance could possibly have been foreseen.

The requirements for membership and transition to a single currency regime are at the center of the Treaty on European Union (TEU). The economic criteria for a country to join appeared quite explicit. First, consumer price inflation could not exceed 1.5 percentage points more than the three best performing countries (Article 1).[2] Second, long-term government bond yields could not exceed two percentage points of the three best performing countries (Article 4). Third, the national currency was required to remain within the rate band of the ERM for two years (Article 3). Most importantly, government budget deficits could not exceed 3% of gross domestic product (GDP) and total government debt was not allowed to exceed 60% of total GDP (Article 1).[3]

Many countries started programs to reform their economies before the Maastricht Treaty even went into force. According to Guldager (1997), most countries that were not meeting the Maastricht criteria made great efforts to reduce their public debt and contain inflation between 1986 and 1990, before the Maastricht period (1992–1998), with the major exception of Greece. Thus, the Maastricht Treaty was requiring changes to the status quo that some countries were making already. There was no "depth" to the commitments states wishing to join EMU were making (Downs *et al.* 1996). But if there was an exogenous shock, noncompliance would be highly likely.

On paper, the TEU appears to have substantially strong enforcement mechanisms. In summary, the Commission, together with ECOFIN (Economic and Financial Committee of the Council of Ministers), would monitor budget situations among eurozone members.[4] If government deficits exceeded these criteria, the Commission would issue an opinion to the EU Council. The Council would then decide, by qualified majority voting, whether an excessive deficit exists and, if so, issue (confidential) policy recommendations to the noncompliant member.[5] The suspect member would then be required to issue reports to the

Council outlining how it was meeting those requirements. If it still failed to comply, the Council would require the offending Member State to publish publicly additional budgetary information before issuing government bonds and securities, making a deposit to the Community of "an appropriate size," and it would impose fines if necessary.[6] The Excessive Deficit Procedure, part of the Growth and Stability Pact (GSP) of 1997, supposedly strengthened the sanctions regime by specifying more clearly the time limits and the sizes of the fines.[7]

Yet the Pact still did not address serious flaws within the eurozone's compliance system. First, there is no independent arbiter, such as the Commission, the ECJ or the European Central Bank (ECB), that is empowered to decide authoritatively whether the criteria are being violated.[8] The Commission can only issue a report to the Council containing its opinion and recommendation. The formal decision to declare a eurozone member not in compliance is left to the Council, placing the decision entirely within the political realm. Even when the Commission attempted to force the Council to take action against Germany and France for excessive deficits in 2003, the ECJ found in favor of the Council.[9] Without an independent arbiter, each eurozone member prefers to ignore the noncompliant behavior of another out of fear that its own violations will be detected and thus face possible retaliation.

Besides insufficient enforcement mechanisms, there were also few mechanisms in place to assist states in meeting their fiscal and monetary obligations. During the negotiations, the French, the Italians and the Commission sought the early establishment of the European Monetary Institute, a precursor to the European Central Bank, sooner rather than later. This would also pressure Germany to address exchange-rate asymmetries and relax its monetary policy, which in turn would make fiscal consolidation among weak currency countries less painful. It would also instill an early commitment to consider other macroeconomic factors, such as unemployment, when the ECB formulated monetary policy. The Germans succeeded in excluding these elements from the agreement.

Germany did agree to additional side-payments to poorer Member States in the form of large increases in structural funds (Moravcsik 1998, Garrett 1992). These were then perceived as side-payments for possible losses other states would incur if they joined the eurozone. But structural funds exist only to foster economic development over the long term. Governments cannot use them to help balance their budgets or respond to changes in the business cycle. The side-payments used to obtain agreement are unrelated to the problems of noncompliance that would occur later.

Once the ECB was set up and EMU began in 1999, efforts to assist countries in complying with the GSP were also prohibited. The strict independence of the ECB prevented it from using monetary easing to support a member's fiscal priorities or macroeconomic conditions. There was also no formal exchange-rate policy, which would help countries deal with balance of payments problems and maintain high levels of exports in the face of currency appreciation. Finally, there were no bailout provisions by the ECB or any other EU institutions in case a country's financial position within the eurozone came under significant international pressure. This portended future crises for the euro.

Finally, despite German efforts, rules specifying both the budgetary criteria and how a noncompliant country would be punished for violating them were still vague. First, it is unclear what "sustainable" public finances or "levels of debt" are when calculating whether the convergence criteria are being violated (Collignon and Mundschenk 1999). Second, euro members were excused from meeting the criteria if the budget deficit exceeded 3 percent of GDP due to "an unusual event outside the control of the Member State" which had a "major" impact on its financial position. Excessive budget deficits were also allowed if they resulted from "a severe economic downturn." The Commission was charged with including these factors among others when issuing its report on compliance. However, little case law or additional legislation exists that defines precisely what these factors are, what weight each factor has, and what degree of consideration each factor should be given when assessing noncompliance. This introduces a great amount of ambiguity as to when the Commission can enforce Maastricht and the Growth and Stability Pact. Third and finally, the entire Excessive Deficit Procedure is written with language that gives the Council members a significant degree of discretion to decide if and when a member has an excessive budget deficit and whether punishment should be meted out.[10]

EMU and the problem of collective action

Noncompliance with the Maastricht Treaty is overdetermined. No one set of factors from any school of thought on compliance explains why noncompliance has occurred. But noncompliance with the Maastricht criteria and the Growth and Stability Pact can also be understood as a problem of collective action (Dyson 2000). When the matter is placed in a collective action framework, we see that the reasons why states do not comply in other situations are also present under EMU. Free riding, threat of mutual retaliation, and asymmetric benefits and costs are all good reasons why noncompliance could have been expected.

Noncompliance in the case of EMU is different from other cases because the costs of noncompliance were large and in the short term, while the benefits were diffused across society and only over the long term. This was at the national level. At the European level, the benefits were concentrated among a few members. There were also strong incentives to free ride. No one state had an incentive to enforce the Treaty's rules upon another. Without any of the compliance mechanisms listed above, the eurozone was ripe for possible collapse if a severe economic shock occurred that threatened the euro's and the regime's stability.

The key public good of EMU was to provide a monetary policy based on "sound money."[11] According to the monetarist school of thought, monetary policy is neutral in terms of its effect on economic growth and employment. Member State governments and influential economists of the time perceived inflation, even at moderate levels, as the main central threat to investment and long-term economic growth. A credible commitment to low inflation reduces uncertainty for international investors, which rewards countries with low long-term interest rates and higher levels of fixed capital investment. The most effective method of demonstrating a strong commitment is the institutionalization of strong, independent central banks (Barro and Gordon 1983). The costs of adjustment, therefore, were left to national governments in the form of reforming their fiscal policies, including their welfare and wage-bargaining systems.

Low inflation in the EU is a pure public good because it is nonexludable and nonrival. As long as the ECB pursued an unaccommodating monetary policy, all Member States would enjoy low premiums on long-term borrowing, whether public or private. Also, no individual member's contribution to the public good is significant enough to affect the provision of the good, with the exception of Germany and perhaps France. As long as the ECB targeted macroeconomic conditions in Germany, other eurozone members would not have to make fiscal adjustments. Acceleration in wage demands, large fiscal deficits, or spikes in overall prices among the smaller eurozone members would not have much determinative effect on ECB's monetary policy decisions.

There is also a large degree of asymmetry within the eurozone in terms of both the capacity and willingness to produce the public good (Verdun 1996). The ability of national governments to change fiscal or wage–labor regimes is shaped by the various institutional structures and obstacles they confront when attempting to implement policy change (Hallerberg 2004, Tsebelis 1995, 1999). In addition, the variety of welfare regimes (Esping-Andersen 1990, Leibfried and Pierson 1995), national taxation regimes (Radaelli 1997) and industrial relations and wage-bargaining systems (Crouch and Streeck 1997, Hall and Soskice 2001) produce the wide variation in interest and capacity that governments have in meeting the Maastricht criteria. Finally, national political parties and voters in different countries have divergent preferences in terms of the tradeoffs they are willing to make between market efficiency and capital investment versus redistribution and the provision of social welfare (Bean *et al.* 1998, Boyer 2000).

These three factors together – limited effect of one member's contribution, asymmetric interests and capacities, and the lack of effective compliance mechanisms – create a recipe for the under-provision of the public good and, therefore, noncompliance. Each member of the eurozone still prefers to create and maintain the euro rather than returning to past monetary arrangements. In addition to producing European monetary stability, the eurozone members had and still have a common vision of a single European currency that sustains the path towards more European integration. This collective interest, as well as other rational incentives, led members to overlook serious cases of noncompliance. For example, the discovery of fraudulent budget statistics for Greece in 2004 exemplifies this pattern.[12] Greece and other countries used creative accounting tools, one-offs and even misreporting to join and remain a eurozone member in good standing (Koen and van den Noord 2005, Von Hagen and Harden 2004). The reluctance that both the ECB and eurozone members had in addressing these problems, hoping they would just disappear, shows the explanatory power of a collective action framework.

Why refusal?

A collective action approach also explains the *type* of noncompliance that occurred. Rather than immediately changing the status quo or delaying until the ECJ issued a final ruling, eurozone members violating the Maastricht criteria simply refused to change the status quo. Noncompliance did not just happen because of a weak institutional regime. Members refused to change the status quo because the costs of policy change were large and spread across society and affected large groups over the long term.

First, as in other cases of noncompliance discussed earlier, the sources of noncompliance emerged because the losers created by the international agreement were not fully compensated. There were winners and losers at both the domestic and the European level. The ECB's monetary policy reflects a commitment to price stability over other macroeconomic factors, such as growth or employment. Those countries in support of more flexible or Keynesian policies, such as France and Italy, lost out. France more or less failed to contain the power of the strong Deutsche mark, spoiling a chance to exert French influence within the EU. The ECB was also not charged with setting a specific exchange rate policy for the euro. As the euro strengthened over time, Italian exports faced greater price competition. With currency devaluation no longer an option, Italian industry faced serious economic difficulties. Some countries' governments also began to fear the "Europeanization" of their own distinct forms of capitalism (see the contributions in Dyson 2002).

The politics of austerity produced by the Maastricht criteria and subsequent Growth and Stability Pact generated growing discontent with the politics of fiscal adjustment, if fiscal reforms happened at all. A strong commitment to reducing budget deficits would lower the wages and the size of the public sector. Trade unions were required to make greater wage concessions, which were not compensated by more generous levels of social spending (Dyson 2000). Consumers and businesses alike faced higher transaction costs, at least over the short term, as governments replaced the national currency with the euro. In some countries, such as Germany and the Netherlands, the conversion rate for the national currency to the euro was set at a level such that consumers perceived that they had lost a large amount of effective buying power.[13]

There were also beneficiaries at the European and national levels. Germany benefitted most from the deal at Maastricht. Since a noninflationary monetary policy rewards economic sectors that export goods of high value and, therefore, skilled workers, Germany benefitted more than others. It also secured greater exchange rate stability on its own terms. The ECB's commitment to a strategy of "sound money" would force national governments to rescale their debt obligations and pursue longer-term, supply-side strategies to create greater economic competitiveness, reflecting Germany's basic macroeconomic policy paradigm.

At the domestic level, international financial markets and transnational corporations benefitted from lower transaction costs by having a single unit of account, albeit once the transition to the euro was completed.[14] With more mobile capital markets that came with the completion of the single market, governments faced a greater risk of tax competition. As a result, the tax burden shifted to employees and consumers and away from capital. Yet, those gains were comparatively low, spread out among many small groups and only realizable far into the future.

Despite the benefits of creating the euro, the seeds of noncompliance lay within the Maastricht Treaty itself. With low benefits concentrated among a few small groups, but large costs spread across society, members had little incentive to comply with EMU criteria. The relatively short history of the euro shows that noncompliance happened frequently.

The box plots in Figure 5.1 show how eurozone members slowly installed fiscal discipline and committed themselves to sound money. During the Maastricht period (1992–98), eurozone members made great efforts to reduce their budget deficits to less than 3 percent GDP (Von Hagen *et al.* 2000). As a result, once the euro was introduced in 1999 as the main unit of account, there was general convergence among eurozone members towards this budgetary rule.

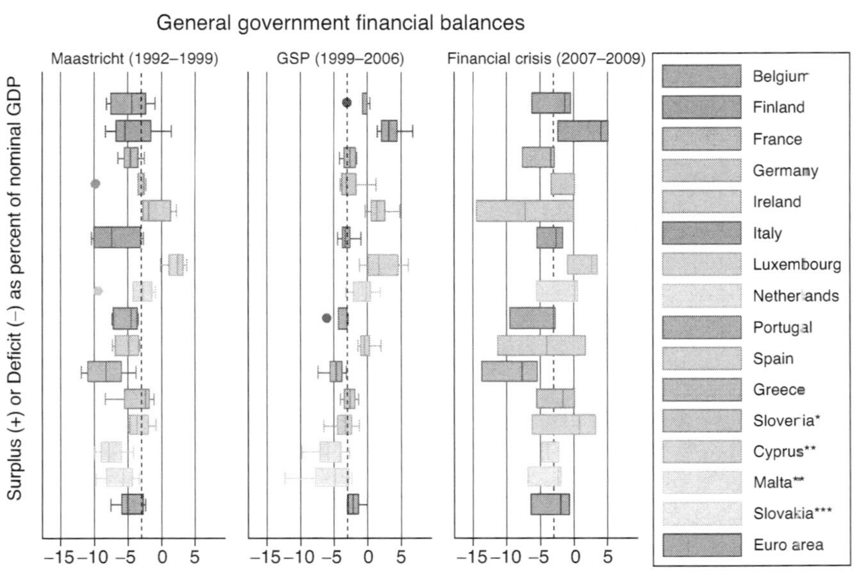

Figure 5.1 Government financial balances.

Source: OECD Economic Outlook 87 database. Joined *2007; ** 2008; ***2009.

During the Maastricht period, most future eurozone members significantly exceeded the 3 percent criteria, but were slowly inching towards compliance by the time the euro was introduced. Once this happened, Member States continued to reduce the size of their budget deficit, although compliance was not perfect. The variation among the eurozone members in the mean size of their budget deficits also decreased, converging towards 3 percent.

In contrast to the budgetary criteria, most eurozone members had already reduced their total debt levels to below the 60 percent threshold. Belgium, Greece and Italy were the only exceptions (see Figure 5.2). These countries continued to make steps towards reducing their total debt. Even though they had not met the necessary criteria, they were permitted to join. However, strict adherence to the Growth and Stability Pact by some members is not the sole explanation for smaller budget deficits and lower overall debt levels. High levels of economic growth in Spain and Ireland, as well as in Luxembourg and Finland, helped these countries' overall fiscal situations. And once economic growth plummeted with the onset of the global financial crisis in 2007, most governments returned to countercyclical fiscal policies that led to violations of the Maastricht criteria.

At the same time, violations of the GSP criteria occurred frequently. Austria, France, Germany, Portugal and Greece all violated euro rules in terms of the sizes of their budget deficits between 1999 and 2006. Despite these violations, not one state was punished for violating the criteria. Even when it was clear that Greece had reportedly falsified budgetary numbers, no action at the EU Council level was taken. Each country knew that its own fiscal policies, budgetary measures

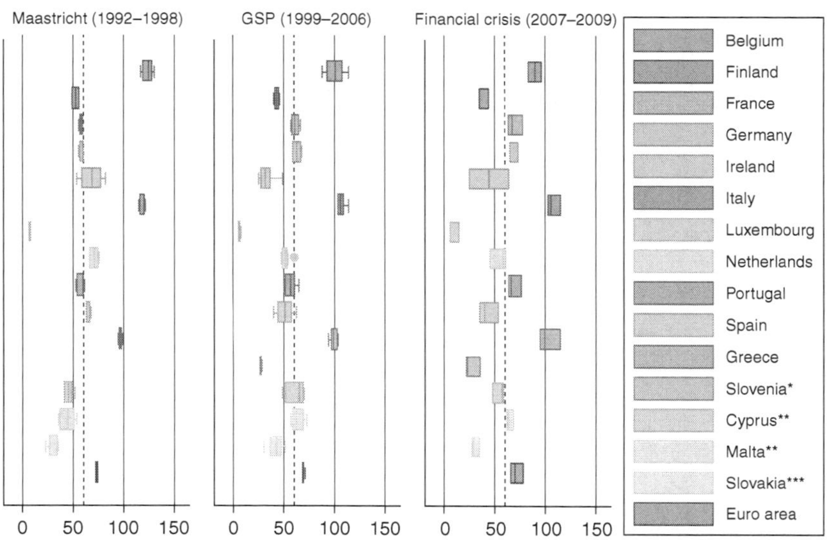

Figure 5.2 Total government debt as percent of GDP.

Source: Eurostat. *Joined 2006; **2007; ***2009.

and creative accounting mechanisms would come under attack in exchange for singling out another member for violating the criteria. In addition, most countries that violated the criteria were small and had no significant impact on the provision of the public good, low inflation and monetary stability.

But when the eurozone faced serious and unanticipated levels of noncompliance by Greece in 2008 and 2009, the weaknesses of EMU were fully exposed to members and nonmembers alike. Greece and other members facing possible default on their public debt confronted a situation in which they once again had to navigate through the Scylla of complying with the eurozone countries' demands and the Charybdis of massive domestic opposition to the required austerity measures. The Greek government and others chose to comply and maintain their membership in the euro. But the ineffectiveness of other eurozone members and the ECB to respond to the Greek financial crisis in its first days raised new questions about the overall desirability of maintaining the euro.

Complying with the eurozone's demands resurrected a long debate over the institutional design of the euro. There were those who argued that it was time that the ECB and its monetary policy served the political demands of its members. It should have an accommodating monetary policy that removed the tight monetary straightjacket on their national budgets. At the same time, there were others who wished to delegate more powers to the ECB to properly manage the euro during such crises. This leads us to one of the most important debates in international relations today, how to establish greater democratic legitimacy for institutions of international governance while maintaining their effectiveness.

Noncompliance, international governance and legitimacy

The difficult choices the Greek government faced in 2009 and 2010 are illustrative of the challenging two-level game policymakers must make when deciding whether or not to comply with international law. They must weigh the benefits of international cooperation over the sometimes-strong opposition of domestic constituencies. Material gains or losses are not the only factors governments are considering. They also face serious issues of legitimacy. Who has authority in situations of noncompliance? Do international legal obligations always trump domestic law when they conflict? Classic normative democratic theory suggests the legitimate authority lies with the people who constitute the government through democratic elections (Schmitter and Karl 1991). But international law also has legitimacy. States are often "pulled" into compliance (Franck 1990, 1995).

Current controversies over the authority of international law and institutions revolve around this issue of which normative obligation deserves greater weight. Some critics argue that both European and international governing institutions suffer from a "democratic deficit." Strengthening the mechanisms for inputting citizens' preferences is the proper prescription. Others argue that if international governing institutions have expanded their authority beyond the control of national governments, then those powers must be returned to the national government. National law should always have precedence over international law. Furthermore, international law has a minimal role in national legal governance. This is an alternative method of maintaining "input" legitimacy.

The scholarly literature on the supposed democratic shortcomings, both normative and empirical, of international and European institutions is vast.[15] The independent power of international institutions, many claim, has grown significantly since the end of the Cold War. The number of institutions, treaties and rules governing state behavior has increased tremendously in the last fifty years.[16] Michael Zürn (2004) argues that the role of international institutions in international relations has also changed qualitatively. These changes are along three dimensions. First, the addressees of international rules are no longer just states, but societal actors as well. Second, international institutions regulate behavior within states, not just activities between them. Third, the complexity of problems international institutions were delegated to solve has also grown substantially.[17] As a consequence, states are demanding more from international institutions in terms of responsibilities and performance (Koremenos *et al.* 2003).

As a result, the argument continues, national governments have lost more authority and control, or national sovereignty. Why have national governments lost control? First, the central locus of decision-making has moved from the national to the international level for functional reasons. Second, the complexity of the problems and the amount of information that international institutions produce regarding these new problems overwhelms parliamentarians.[18] Third, in many situations, a type of "slack" often develops when principals delegate more powers to agents (Pollack 1997). Agents, seeking more autonomy and powers, can escape the supervision of their principals. As a result, international institutions accumulate more power and authority than was originally intended.

First, let us consider whether there is a problem of democratic legitimacy at all. Some scholars are not yet prepared to make the leap that the delegation of these powers to international institutions, such as the European Commission and ECJ, has necessarily led to less accountability. First, they argue, international law and institutions do no more, and sometimes less, than what their members demand of them (Goldsmith and Posner 2005). Andrew Moravcsik's claim that no democratic deficit exists in the EU mirrors this chain of argument. Similarly, Majone (2005) argues that EU institutions exist to solve regulatory conflicts and that a certain degree of autonomy from majoritarian institutions is necessary (Majone 1996, 2005).

If Member States are adequate at controlling how much authority and control international institutions accumulate, then we would expect that the ECJ would rarely issue decisions that threaten vital national interests (Garrett 1995). If they do, according to the rationalist school, we should observe states refusing to comply all of the time unless it is in their interests to do so.[19] The case studies that make up this study show that governments are reluctant to comply when the costs are prohibitively large and spread across society.[20] Governments are willing to comply with the demands of international courts when the costs are low and concentrated among a few small groups. They are rarely willing to sacrifice the long-term and substantial gains generated by international cooperation in favor of satisfying a powerful domestic constituency.

From this perspective, the dangers of undemocratic international governance are exaggerated. In addition, the claim that domestic actors, such as national parliamentarians, are so overwhelmed by information, or deal with information asymmetries that international institutions can gain greater autonomy as a result, is also somewhat exaggerated. Parliamentarians are not the only actors that can monitor when international institutions are overstepping their authority. Losers, I have argued, are more likely to monitor the effects of international agreements than winners. They have stronger incentives to manage a government's decision to comply with international law. Some actors are not just concerned with the material effects of compliance. They are also wary of the new powers that international institutions, such as courts, may accrue as a result of compliance litigation. For example, when the ECJ first began hearing cases related to violations of EU law, it did not just issue an independent judgment about what constituted compliance. It also assumed more authority by asserting that EU law had precedence over national law.[21] In the United States, even if compliance will arguably improve the status quo by reducing security threats or enhancing economic welfare, many conservative legal scholars are skeptical of international law's place in the American constitutional legal order.

Actors who oppose compliance can reduce the amount of information asymmetry between domestic actors and international institutions and reduce the chances of international expanding their authority of national governments. Also, national politicians are also careful not to underestimate the amount of domestic opposition to compliance that can also accumulate over time. Assuming that government officials are most concerned about being re-elected, they might just as likely be cautious about delegating more authority to international institutions as wanting to secure the future gains of international cooperation.

But there are also good rational reasons for why not to underestimate the possibility of a democratic deficit emerging. The arguments above assume perfect information. Citizens and parliamentarians alike are also not able to calculate accurately all of the consequences of a new international rule, if they are aware of them at all. They are also rationally ignorant about EU and international affairs. Voters choose not to focus on international affairs because the issues are complex. It is difficult to assign blame or credit for policy reform or economic conditions to remote institutions rather than national politicians. And these issues are not of a high priority among voters' concerns.[22] Furthermore, national political debates during elections rarely center on issues related to foreign affairs.[23] Even in the EU, where intervention by EU institutions into national affairs is an accepted part of political reality by now, EU-related issues rarely become the focus of national discourse. European parties rarely take clear positions on compliance or the amount of authority EU institutions have been delegated.

Moreover, since international cooperation is a public good, the gains are relatively diffuse across a large part of national society. International or EU affairs are not just remote or have little saliency. They also involve gains or losses that are of a minimal nature. Of all of the other issues voters and citizens care about when participating in politics, the relatively legitimacy of international law and its impact on democratic governance does not rank high on that list.

Debates over how much power international or European institutions have do not become salient until voters have an opportunity to vote directly on them, such as during the recent referenda on the European Constitution. And the results were problematic for the future of the EU (Bailey 2008). But such opportunities are rare in the European Union. They are also rare in other countries when the authority of international institutions comes into question.

Thus, while there are strong arguments from the rationalist school for why no democratic deficit exists in the EU or between governments and other international regimes, there are also strong rationalist arguments for the opposite. Making the more realistic assumption of imperfect information and rational ignorance of international issues allows us to conclude that the ability of international institutions to overstep their authority is a strong possibility. There are also arguments for why international institutions are able to overstep the bounds of their delegated authority. The demand to do so also comes from national governments themselves.

Governments must weigh the domestic costs of noncompliance over forgoing the benefits of cooperation. States are sometimes required to comply in order to produce the public good. In addition, they may comply in order to demonstrate they are reliable partners and achieve the future gains of cooperation. A regime member also wants to avoid punishment if found to be noncompliant. If national politicians know that electoral punishment is not likely to materialize, then governments are likely to delegate more governance responsibilities to international institutions to solve complex problems.

These arguments for why international institutions assume ever more power are also fully consistent with a social constructivist approach to international law. As discussed in the social constructivist literature, states comply because international law possesses a legitimate pull of its own. In the EU, the pull of legitimacy is strongest among international regimes. For example, EU law is now part of a Member State's national legal order. As a result, when cases of noncompliance occur, national governments comply not because it is in their interest, but because it constitutes appropriate behavior in a political regime defined by the rule of law. Member State governments may choose to defend the current status quo because a strong domestic group opposes it or because the legal principle and its implications are still undefined or vague. However, governments do acknowledge the legitimacy and authority international institutions have, especially international courts, for a variety of reasons.[24] Once the legal issue is clarified or further noncompliance would violate the normative prescription for a Member State to satisfy its legal obligations, national governments usually choose to change the status quo. This may explain why cases of complete refusal are rare in the EU among all of the violations that members commit and heard by the ECJ, even if the required changes are minimal.

Whether in the EU or in the international system in general, international courts have their own sources of legitimacy. They may not have armies to enforce it decisions, as President Jackson famously stated after the US Supreme Court's decision that removal of the Cherokee Indians from Georgia was illegal.[25] But, just as constitutional courts enjoy legitimacy in national democracies, so do international law and international legal institutions among governments. The independent power of international institutions and law to pull states into compliance is well documented (Alter 2003, 2008). As the body of international law grows and levels of legalization increase, the authority and powers of international institutions increase as well. This depends, of course, on the nature of the legal disputes themselves. Not every case before an independent tribunal chooses to address involves the scope of its authority. But, if we assume that international institutions always strive for more authority and power in order to expand their role in international society and use the law to achieve that goal, then they can accrue greater responsibilities as regime members follow somewhat reluctantly by satisfying their international legal obligations.

Conservative legal scholars are both extremely concerned about these developments and adamantly opposed to them (Posner 2009; Rabkin 2005). They argue that international law has limited authority of its own. It should only be complied with, they argue, when it is directly in the interests of the state to do so. Their views are parallel to the growing opposition to international institutions and their power among rightist groups in both Europe and the United States.

Conservative legal criticism bemoans the presence of international law in national political systems for many reasons. Among them is the fact that international law is divorced from a nation's constitutional identity (Rabkin 2005). In contrast, criticisms usually from the Left bemoan the absence of effective mechanisms to make international governance more democratic, and not necessarily the power of international law in national society (Slaughter 2004). What both perspectives ignore is the other dimension of legitimacy, which is legitimacy of the output international institutions and law produces. Democratic institutions at any level of governance are not just judged by how well they incorporate the preferences of their constituents. They are also judged according to how well they perform (Diamond 1999). Democratic procedures mean little if these institutions are not effectively providing public goods. Domestic or international institutions are also legitimate if they perform core functions. This is "output" legitimacy.

Solving the shortcomings in one form of legitimacy may affect the other. In short, there may be a trade-off between improving the "democratic-ness" of international governance and its actual performance in solving current problems of collective action or the reasons why states cooperate in the first place. Compliance with international law generates questions about not just whether there is a trade off between input and output legitimacy. As with other nondemocratic, non-majoritarian institutions, there must be. What is more important for both researchers and citizens is to determine what that trade-off looks like in different institutional settings, how that trade-off is reached, and whether those solutions are satisfactory in terms of having both input and output legitimacy.

On the one hand, increasing input legitimacy of international institutions can harm their effectiveness. Assume that international institutions are redesigned to include important mechanisms that enhance democratic legitimacy. They allow citizens to participate more, engage in deliberation or the ties of representation are strengthened. As institutions are redesigned with new, more democratic procedures, the efficiency of international institutions in reaching decisions can decline. This has been one of the main critiques of the governance process in the EU. Decision-making in the EU has become so complex and cumbersome that it cannot respond to crises. And the mechanisms are so opaque that it becomes difficult to attribute responsibility or blame for specific policies adopted.

Conversely, let us also assume that the scope of authority of international institutions is curtailed such that democratic parliaments maintain supremacy. In all or most cases in which there are conflicts between a government's international legal obligations and the status quo, governments are required not to comply. While national governments may be satisfying their obligation to privilege national constitutional law over international law, they also jeopardize the likelihood that the gains of international cooperation will be achieved. Independent tribunals are established to improve the chances of cooperation by adjudicating disputes between members. The more restricted international courts and law is the less likely additional cooperation can be achieved in the future or respond to unanticipated threats to international cooperation. If true, international institutions may lose this dimension of their legitimacy, which is generating an output that national governments demand of it (Scharpf 1999). As in national democracies, international institutions do not just possess legitimacy in terms of how well they include the preferences of their constituents into the process of governance. They also gain legitimacy in that they perform essential functions.

Governmental leaders are caught in a serious tradeoff between producing real change that arguably improves the world for most people and yet remaining as democratically accountable as possible. International institutions must be able to effectively fulfill the demands of their constituents and react as well to new, unanticipated challenges. The EU's inability to respond adequately for months to the Greek financial crisis is a good example. Criticism abounds also over the procedures and rules that shape how the ECB makes monetary policy. The ECB is the epitome of an undemocratic institution. It is not allowed to take into the political demands of eurozone members when crafting monetary policy. Its independence from political demands, some argue, is a necessary condition for it to produce the European public good of price stability. Furthermore, some argue that because the ECB lacked the appropriate powers to act decisively to contain the Greek debt crisis is one reason why the euro faced the most serious challenge to its existence since its arrival in 1999.

If the procedures governing monetary policy and financial stability were made more democratic and included the consent of domestic actors, then the ability of the ability of the ECB to react quickly to the crisis would also have been placed in jeopardy. The inability of the eurozone Member States to respond quickly and adequately to the Greek debt crisis shows the perils of increasing an international institution's "democratic-ness." The divergent preferences of the Member States' preferences would only have delayed action further.

The ECB's inability to manage the debt loads of eurozone members and ensure compliance with the Maastricht criteria because of the members' demands that the ECB not interfere in a state's fiscal policy prevented it from adequately responding to the crisis. Therefore, from both perspectives, if the ECB either became more democratic or had its power to intervene in national affairs more restricted, the public good of financial stability in the EU would be placed in jeopardy, which clearly was the case.

There are no easy answers as to how to strike the right balance between "input" and "output" legitimacy. Effective solutions to many of the problems governments face today require international cooperation. Transnational terrorism and climate change are just two examples of how international cooperation is required to abate their threats. But, inevitably, conditions will arise when doing so imposes some substantial costs on one member of a regime. Industries will not be allowed to pollute. Crucial political supporters could be punished. In Europe, the struggle over finding the balance between sustaining the gains generated by European integration and addressing issues related to a democratic deficit will continue. Much like Homer's Odysseus, European governments will continue struggling to navigate between the Scylla of unaccountable governance by EU institutions and the Charybdis of domestic backlash while sailing the straits of European integration that began at Messina.

Notes

1 Introduction

1 The literature on two-level games is extensive. A small sampling includes Dai (2007), Evans *et al.* (1993), Iida (1993), Milner and Rosendorff (1997), Mo (1995) and Putnam (1988).

2 Downs and Jones (2002) discuss the differences between reputation and reciprocation, but they overlap significantly. See also Guzman (2008).

3 To avoid confusion, this book will use the article numbering contained in the "Treaty on the Functioning of the European Union," consolidated by the Treaty of Lisbon of 2009.

2 A theory of noncompliance

1 For an example of when states actually conclude agreements that make some worse off, see Gruber (2000).

2 For the debate over whether states are driven more by absolute or relative gains, see Snidal (1991).

3 See, for example, Maduro (1998) for the development of law related to the free movement of goods. See also works by Joseph H.H. Weiler (1991, 1994, 1999) for how and why the EU developed a supranational legal authority.

4 Not all international agreements qualify as public goods. Some are club goods, by which the benefits produced accrue only to the members of the regime, such as bilateral treaties or belonging to the World Bank.

5 There seems to be little evidence of how much Czechoslovakia and other communist countries failed to meet their obligations on the Sulfur Protocol aside from her remark that "Consistent with such weak support for sulfur reduction policies, Czechoslovakia was still quite some distance away from the minimum compliance requirement right to the time of the separation of the two Republics" (Dai 2007: 98).

6 In her case studies, Dai does show that major industries, especially in the former communist countries, opposed complying with the Sulfur Protocol (Dai 2007: 97–98).

7 The theoretical framework presented here is significantly derived from Lisa Conant's masterful study of comparative policy change caused by European legal integration. Conant (2002) chooses to focus on how policy change occurs through the variable ability and willingness of domestic groups to cause national policy change by using EU law against their own national governments. The present study in noncompliance can be considered to be a companion to Conant's analysis. While she focuses on domestic interests unsatisfied with the policy status quo, my study concentrates on actual behavior that is outright incongruent with an international rule. But whether significant policy change results from changing noncompliance behavior is outside the scope of this book.

8 Of course, there are wider implications for a conflict-ridden society if war criminals are brought to trial and convicted.
9 This might especially be the case in the United States (Posner 2009, Rabkin 2005).
10 *George W Bush v. Al Gore*, 531 U.S. 9898 (2000); *Hamdan v. Rumsfeld*, 548 U.S. 557 (2006).
11 President Andrew Jackson allegedly made this comment after the US Supreme Court ruled in *Worcester v. Georgia* that the U.S. state of Georgia could not impose its laws on Cherokee lands.
12 Again, this assumes that a signatory to the agreement could not obtain significant protections or side-payments to avoid making changes to the status quo that would harm domestic groups.
13 See the contributions in Rometsch and Wessels (1996).
14 For example, states making agreements that may make them worse off (see Gruber 2000).
15 This argument is derived from George Tsebelis's work using spatial theory to explain policy change (Tsebelis 1999, 2002).
16 One possible exception could include the sanctioning of Austria when the Freedom Party of Austria (FPÖ) became part of the governing coalition. Yet, there are disputes over the relative effectiveness of the "shunning" techniques other Member States used (Merlingen *et al.* 2001).
17 Even if the EU can still be considered a typical international institution.
18 See, among many other works, the contributions in Cowles *et al.* (2001) and Featherstone and Radaelli (2003).

3 Noncompliance and national tradition: enforcing the free movement of goods in Germany and France

1 For example, see Mazzucelli (1999).
2 Moravscik (1998) discounts both of these reasons for European integration.
3 In 1991, the Maastricht Treaty or Treaty of European Union added two additional titles to facilitate the free movement of goods.
4 Article 30 contains an additional clause that did not just remove all specific duties and charges on products among the Member States. It also states that "all measures of equivalent effect" were to be abolished as well. This clause was subsequently used by the ECJ, together with the Commission, to attack all types of charges, fees or costs that could possibly be imposed by national governments, often for innocuous reasons or that of minimal effect. In addition to Article 30, Article 110 seeks to prevent the Member States from transforming charges on foreign products into discriminatory forms of internal discrimination. Also vital to the establishment of the customs union, and later the common market, was the free flow of goods and services from third countries once they have entered the EU and have been charged the appropriate duties and fees, as stipulated in Article 31.
5 Besides Article 36, which is discussed below, the final article listed under Title 1 of the EC Treaty addresses state monopolies and introduces prohibitions against any discriminatory policies that affect the procurement or marketing of goods among Member States. Since this article and its legal implementation fall under issues dealing primarily with competition policy, we can ignore this item for now.
6 *Van Gend en Loos v. Nederlandse Administratie der Belastigen*, Case 26/62, [1963] ECR 1.
7 *Costa v. Ente Nazionale per l'Energia Elettrica (ENEL)*, Case 6/64, [1964] ECR 585.
8 *Amministrazione delle Finanze Dello Stato v. Simmenthal SpA*, Case 106/77, [1978] ECR 629.

9 The free movement of goods is only one component of the four "freedoms" that constitute the internal market, which also include the free movement of workers, capital, and services. In these cases, however, the use of directives rather than direct enforcement by the Commission and the ECJ has been the primary method to achieve market harmonization.
10 Article 36, Treaty on the Functioning of the European Union.
11 *Commission v. Italy* [1969] ECR 193.
12 *Procureur v. Dassonville* [1974] 837.
13 *Rewe-Zentral v. Bundesmonopolverwaltung für Branntwein*, Case 120/78, [1979] ECR 649.
14 *Bodin v. Mingeut*, Case 241/86, [1987] ECR 2573.
15 *Torfaen Borough Council v. B & Q PLC*, Case C-145/88, [1989] ECR 3851.
16 *Keck and Mithouard*, Cases C-267 & 268/91, [1993] ECR I-6097.
17 It is now confirmed that the Bavarian *Reinheitsgebot* is not the first beer purity regulation in Germany. Rather, the first such regulation was discovered in 2001 in the state archives of Weimar, dating back to 1348. While often cited as one of the world's earliest health laws, another persuasive rationale for the law argues that wheat was formally excluded to save it for bread production (Opinion of Advocate General Slynn in Case 178/84, see below).
18 See §§ 9–10 of the *Biersteuergesetz* (BstG), BGBI 1952, p. 149.
19 Any beer that did not contain these four ingredients, or contained additional ones besides these four, was required to be labeled an "alcohol-containing fermented soft drink" (*Frankfurter Rundschau*, May 10, 1986, p. 5).
20 Source: Deutscher Brauer-Bund, e.V., 2006. The fact that revenues have continued to increase in Bavaria while the number of breweries has decreased illustrates the effect of consolidation.
21 Germany did not defend the BStG under Article 36, because it argued that the law did not violate Article 34.
22 Furthermore, Germany's argument about the need to protect its citizens' health was not viewed as credible given that it allowed beer exported from Germany to other Member States to contain additional additives, thereby insinuating that the health of other Europeans was less important than that of the health of its own citizens.
23 Court Opinion, *Commission v. Germany*, Case 178/84, [1987] ECR 1227.
24 Verordnung des Bundesministers für Jugend, Familie, Frauen und Gesundheit, Drucksache 277/90, April 18, 1990.
25 European Commission, Infraction fiche: 19900414.
26 Verordnung des Bundesministeriums für Gesundheit, Drucksache 378/93, May 27, 1993.
27 Verordnung des Bundesministeriums für Gesundheit, Drucksache 749/95, November 3, 1995.
28 EC Decision 292/1997. The list of "traditional national specialties" includes: beer, chocolate, confectionery, pasta, pre-cooked meals, prepared condiment sauces, soups or broths, beverages made from plant extracts, and ice creams or sorbets.
29 While the German *Reinheitsgebot* obtained protective status at the European level, a brewery in Frankfurt an der Order successfully sued officials in the Federal Administrative Court in the Land of Brandenburg in 2005 so that it could continue to produce and sell beer that did not comply with the *Reinheitsgebot* (*Stuttgarter Nachrichten*, February 25, 2005).
30 In 1895, Auguste and Louis Lumière held the first screening of a moving image with their new, dual-purpose camera-projector, or *cinématographe*. Less controversial is the establishment of major film production companies first in France, including the Pathé Frères film company in 1896 and Léon Gaumont, who launched the first movie studios for film production and distribution (Hayward 2000: 195–196).

31 The English title is “Merry Christmas, Mr. Lawrence,” directed by Nagisa Ohima (1983) and features David Bowie.

32 The *Cinéthèque SA* case, 60/1984, was joined by Case 61/1984, *Editions Renée Chateau SARL, Hollywood Boulevard Diffusion—Michael Fabre and DGD SPRL v. FNCA*. Cerito Films and Films Ariane granted Renée Chateau SARL the exclusive rights to distribute the film, “Le Marginal,” on videocassette, while Hollywood Boulevard was granted a performance certificate to show the film in cinemas, in order to counteract the growth in pirated videocassettes. They also sought a suspension of the decree that halted the distribution of videocassettes in place as a result of the initiative of FNCA.

33 Cases 60 & 61/84 *Cinéthèque SA* [1985] ECR 2605, [1986] 1 CMLR 365.

34 In fact, since the *compte de soutien*, which taxes total box-office receipts, and the *taxe spéciale additionnelle* (TSA), which taxes cinemas a certain percentage receiving state funding, the growing popularity of American films would only increase tax revenues and, thereby, financial support for French cinema.

35 Counting which films are “French” is problematic. First, the French government can support films that are made by French directors but performed in English, feature non-French actors, or are co-productions with other countries, which are covering a majority share of total production costs. Also, as Gordon and Meunier (2001) argue, only a few French films account for most of the total box-office receipts of French-made films, such as *Le Dîner de Cons*, *Les Visiteurs 2*, and *Taxi*. However, this pattern is no different from the American movie market, where a few films always account for a large percentage of total box-office receipts each year.

36 Source: www.cnc.fr (accessed March 31, 2010).

37 For example, between 1986 and 2008, *SOFICA* contributions for French film initiatives climbed from €17.5 to €38.3, but the percentage of total film costs for film production covered by these funds declined from approximately 20 per cent to 4.8 per cent. Overall French financial support of the industry continued to increase, mainly because of increasing box office receipts, but the proportion of total film production costs covered by these subsidies declined considerably.

38 See *R. v The Pharmaceutical Society of Great Britain, ex parte the Association of Pharmaceutical Importers (API)*, [1987] 3 CMLR 951.

4 Stopping state rescues: complying with EU state aid policy in Germany and the United Kingdom

1 State aid policy is a poor cousin compared to the other elements of competition policy. They include the regulation of firms that engage in unfair and uncompetitive business practices, limit competition through agreement with other firms (horizontal agreements) or, by controlling firms along different links in the chain of production (vertical agreements) (Article 101 TFEU), act as monopolies or abuse of one’s dominant position (Article 102 TFEU). Regulating these activities among private firms in the EU lies at the core of DGIV’s mission.

2 Case 730/79 *Philip Morris Holland B.V. v. EC Commission* [1980] ECR 2671.

3 Case 142/87 *Commission v. Belgium* [1990] ECR I-959.

4 Case C-75/97 *Belgium v. Commission* [1999] ECR I-3671.

5 Case C-280/00 *Altmark Trans GmbH, Regierungspräsidium Magdeburg v. Nahverkehrsgesellschaft Altmark GmbH* [2003].

6 Commission reports on noncompliance suffer from inconsistent methodologies (Schütterle 2003). However, comparisons can still be made using the data available within individual reports.

7 EU State Aid Reports and Scorecards.

8 The cooperative banks are organized in a similar way. Decentralized according to Land, these banks act as cooperatives for specific segments of the German economy by

providing them with short-term loans and other special services under German law (Deeg 1999: 30).

9 Calculations by Deeg (1999): 83.

10 In 2009 Commerzbank acquired Dresdner Bank.

11 Who actually owns these banks is uncertain and has significantly changed over time.

12 There are federal equivalents to the development banking activities of the Landesbanken.

13 This excludes the large amount of legal scholarship that has studied the WestLB case.

14 Directives 89/647 and Directive 92/121.

15 The facility for individual firms to notify the Commission of a suspected violation was not possible before Regulation No. 659/1999 of 22 March 1999, which laid down detailed rules for the application of Article 93 (now Art. 88). *Official Journal,* L 83/1, 27.03.1999.

16 Case T-223/99, filed on 12 October 1999.

17 Case T-228/99.

18 Grossman (2006) provides an excellent review of the historical record of how the second WestLB came about (Grossman 2006: 336).

19 Commission Decision 3528/2007 of July 18, 2007.

20 Commission Decision 4196/2010 of June 22, 2010.

21 See Judgment of the Court of First Instance in Joined Cases T-228/99 and T-223/99. WestLB then subsequently sued the Commission for recovery of their legal fees and expenses, which they claimed amount to over €3 billion. The European Court of Justice awarded only €353,300 (see Judgment of the European Court of Justice, Case T-228/99, December 19, 2006).

22 See sources in Grossman (2006): 339.

23 Alasdair Murray, "German economic model threatened," *The Times (London)*, January 12, 2000.

24 Ian Fraser, Patrick Hosking and Allan Hall, "Keeping Kirch on the Pitch," *The Sunday Herald*, February 24, 2002.

25 See sources in Smith (2001): 530.

26 WestLB itself began to orientate itself outwards and engage international securities markets.

27 DTI was renamed and replaced with the Department of Business, Enterprise and Regulatory Reform in 2007, which was disbanded and made part of the Department for Business, Innovation and Skills in 2009.

28 The group also contained a trucks division, which was sold off to a Dutch firm in 1982. In 1984 Jaguar became independent through a public sale of shares and was purchased by Ford. BL also owned the MG brand, which returned to the international market upon the sale of the Rover Group to Nanjing Motors by BMW in 2005.

29 The sale of BL's assets to either GM or Ford took place in an atmosphere already polluted by acrimony over the sale of Westland, Britain's last helicopter manufacturer, in January of 1986. Then-Defense Minister Heseltine preferred merging Westland with its European counterparts, while No.10 Downing Street's and Westland's management favored a deal with America's Sikorsky. Heseltine's refusal to follow Thatcher's wishes and decision to lead internal correspondence led to his resignation and, later, that of Sir Leon Brittan of DTI as well.

30 Michael Smith and John Palmer, "BAe Snaps Up Rover for 150 million pounds," *The Guardian (London), March 30, 1988*.

31 Commission Decision 89/58/EEC, Official Journal L 025, 28/01/1989, pp. 92–100.

32 Her charms were likely to fail after she "embarrassed" President Delors at the London EEC Summit in 1986 and since she bypassed Commissioner Sutherland completely by appealing directly to Delors (Richard Owen, "Rover-BAe Merger Faces a Bumpy Ride," *The Times (London), June 18, 1988).*

33 Robin Oakley and Daniel War, "Ministers Baffled At Rover Deal Hitch." *The Times (London), July 14, 1988.*
34 BAe would save £22 million by deferring the £150 payment of the sale to the Treasury by 20 months. In addition, BAe would receive £3 million for investment in a planned subscription to the European Columbus space project, £9.5 million to buy out the remaining private shareholders, and £11 million to cover the costs of the sale.
35 John Bourn of the Comptroller and Auditor General of DTI prepared the memos for the Commons public accounts committee.
36 Anonymous Byline, "Government 'tried to deceive:' Rover takeover; Parliament." *The Times (London), December 14, 1989.*
37 Stephen Goodwin, "Parliament and Politics: Taxpayers 'swindled over Rover sale'." *The Independent, December 1, 1989.*
38 Ibid.
39 Michael Binyon, "Brittan Tells Government to Recover Illegal £44 million." *The Times (London), June 28, 1990.*

5 Conclusion

1 Besides Andrew Moravcsik's exegesis (Moravcsik 1998: Chapter 6), there is Kenneth Dyson and Kevin Featherstone's (1999) comprehensive account.
2 All Article numbers refer to Protocol No. 13 on the Convergence Criteria attached to the TFEU.
3 Protocol No. 10 on the Excessive Deficit Procedure.
4 Article 126(2,3) TFEU.
5 Article 126(8,13) TFEU.
6 Article 126(11c,d) TFEU.
7 Council Regulation No. 1467/97 of 7 July 1997 [OJ L 209 of 2 August 1997]. Germany insisted at various times during the negotiation process that sanctions be coupled with the withholding of EC funds, prosecution by the Commission, suspension of EC membership, all by simple majority in the Council (Moravcsik 1998: 445).
8 The Commission is not allowed to prosecute noncompliant members, and Articles 258 and 259 TFEU, which allow either the Commission or another Member State to bring a possible violation before the European Court of Justice, are explicitly excluded from the process of bringing states into compliance with the Growth and Stability Pact.
9 *Commission v. Council*, Case C-27/2004, ECR-I 06649.
10 For example, the Council's decision to give formal notice and sanction an offending Member states: "The Council *may* give notice to the Member State concerned to take measures to reduce the deficit. … No later than four months after the notice has been given, the Council *normally* decides to impose sanctions if the Member State fails to comply with the Council's decisions. … *In principle*, the interval between the reporting of the figures indicating that an excessive deficit exists and the decision to impose sanctions should not exceed sixteen months" (italics added)."
11 For the role of these economic ideas throughout the history of European monetary integration, see McNamara (1998).
12 Almost every country engaged in the use of "creative accounting" to join and remain a member of the eurozone. Almost all countries used various budgetary and accounting devices in order to comply with the Excessive Deficit Procedure (see Ohlsson 2007).
13 Although the German public and politicians perceived that the euro had caused severe price hikes, there is no statistical evidence to support that claim (Brachinger 2006). The rejection of the EU Constitution in the Netherlands is also attributed to the Dutch public's perception that the euro introduced price inflation (Aarts and Kolk 2006).
14 The size of these gains can be disputed as most transnational corporations used derivatives and other financial instruments to hedge against exchange risk (Cohen 2003).

15 The literature on the hypothesized democratic deficit in the EU has grown substantially in recent years. For a cogent analysis of the debate, both normatively and empirically, see Schmidt (2006). The contributions in Kohler-Koch and Rittberger (2007) address a variety of dimensions associated with the debate over the democratic deficit. For an introduction to the debate over the democratic legitimacy of international law, see Wheatley (2010) and the contributions in Fox and Roth (2000).

16 The number of international agreements in existence climbed from 15,000 in 1960 to 55,000 in 1997, based on statistics from the World Treaty Index (Zürn 2004: 267).

17 One objection to each of these claims is that international agreements always possessed these qualities. The distinction between inter- and intra-state issues is difficult to discern. Whether it is how borders are patrolled or restrictions on the use of forces, there are domestic groups that win or lose from the enforcement of these rules. As a result, international rules have always indirectly addressed societal behavior, if not formally and legally, and have affected domestic regulatory behavior. Finally, Zürn (2004) does not explicate why we should assume that the complexity of problems that need solving has increased over time. Regulating financial flows and exchange rates under Bretton Woods can be as vexing as solving issues related to international finance today.

18 Even with this argument, we need a comparative analysis to assess whether national parliamentarians are more overwhelmed with technical problems than they were when international institutions were delegated fewer powers. There are good reasons to suspect not.

19 Or, as we witnessed in Garrett's analysis of the *Cinématique* decision, rationalist scholars assume that any decision the ECJ reaches in a case of noncompliance must reflect the interests of a Member State, based on the fear of backlash by it and other EU members.

20 Similarly, Zürn's (2004) discussion of German and French noncompliance with EU rules during the 1999 BSE crisis shows some of the similar dynamics to those that occurred under EMU.

21 This is part of the long constitutional history of EU law Joseph H. H. Weiler (1982, 1994).

22 One exception may be the rule of the IMF during national debt crises. The IMF's demands that austerity measures be introduced led to riots across numerous countries John Walton and Charles Ragin, "Global and National Sources of Political Protest: Third World Responses to the Debt Crisis," *American Sociological Review* 55, no. 6 (1990).

23 To be clear, I argue only that these particular issues, where does sovereignty lie, are questions that voters do not give primacy when entering the voting booth. Voters are able to formulate relatively rational attitudes related to developments in foreign affairs (Holsti 1996). They also hold their representatives to account for failure or success (Aldrich et al. 1989). But such moments of accountability only happen when issues of foreign affairs become relatively salient, such as during war. Therefore, it is unlikely that issue related to the sovereignty of national governments under international law are important drivers of public opinion, even in the European Union.

24 See Chapter 1.

25 *Worcester v. Georgia* 31 US (6 Pet.) 515 (1832).

Bibliography

Aarts, K. and Kolk, V. D. (2006) Understanding the Dutch "No": The Euro, the East, and the Elite. *PS: Political Science and Politics*, 39, 243–246.

Abbott, F. (2000) NAFTA and the Legalization of World Politics. *International Organization*, 54, 519–548.

Abbott, K. W. and Snidal, D. (1998) Why States Act through Formal International Organizations. *Journal of Conflict Resolution*, 42, 3–32.

Abbott, K. W., Keohane, R. O., Moravcsik, A., Slaughter, A.-M. and Snidal, D. (2001) The Concept of Legalization. In Goldstein, J., Kahler, M., Keohane, R. and Slaughter, A.-M. (Eds.) *Legalization and World Politics*. Cambridge, MA, The MIT Press.

Aldrich, J., Sullivan, J. and Borgida, E. (1989) Foreign Affairs and Issue Voting: Do Presidential Candidates 'Waltz before a Blind Audience?' *American Political Science Review*, 83(1), 123–141.

Allen, C. S. (1989) The Underdevelopment of Keynesianism in the Federal Republic of Germany. In Hall, P. A. (Ed.) *The Political Power of Economic Ideas*. Princeton, NJ, Princeton University Press.

Alter, K. (2001) *Establishing the Supremacy of European Law*. Oxford, Oxford University Press.

Alter, K. (2003) Do International Courts Enhance Compliance with International Law? *Review of Asian and Pacific Studies*, 25, 51–78.

Alter, K. (2008) Agents or Trustees? International Courts in their Political Contexts. *European Journal of International Relations*, 14, 33–63.

Alter, K. and Vargas, J. (2000) Explaining Variation in the Use of European Litigation Strategies: European Community Law and British Gender Equality Policy. *Comparative Political Studies*, 33, 452–482.

Axelrod, R. (1984) *Evolution of Cooperation*. New York, Basic Books.

Axelrod, R. and Keohane, R. (1985) Achieving Cooperation under Anarchy: Strategies and Institutions. *World Politics*, 38, 226–254.

Bailer, S. and Schneider, G. (2006) Nash versus Schelling? The Importance of Constraints in Legislative Bargaining. In Thomson, R., Stokman, F. N., Achen, C. and König, T. (Eds.). Oxford, UK, Oxford University Press.

Bailey, D. J. (2008) Misperceiving The European Union Decides: Testing Theories of European Decision-Making Matters: Elite Ideas and the Failure of the Constitution. *Comparative European Politics*, 6, 33–60.

Balme, R. and Woll, C. (2005) France: Between Integration and Sovereignty. In Bulmer, S. and Lequesne, C. (Eds.) *The Member States of the European Union*. Oxford, UK, Oxford University Press.

Barnett, M. N. and Finnemore, M. (1999) The Politics, Power and Pathologies of International Organizations. *International Organization*, 53, 699–732.

Barro, R. J. and Gordon, D. B. (1983) A Critical Theory of Monetary Policy in a National Rate Model. *Journal of Political Economy*, 91, 589–610.

Baun, M. J. (1995) The Maastricht Treaty as High Politics: Germany, France, and European Integration. *Political Science Quarterly*, 110, 605–624.

Baun, M. J. (1996) *An Imperfect Union: The Maastricht Treaty and the New Politics of European Integration.* London, Westview Press.

Bean, C., Bentolila, S., Bertola, G. and Dolado, J. (1998) *Social Europe: One for All?* London, Centre for Economic Policy Research.

Berkeley, N., Donnelly, T., Morris, D. and Donnelly, M. (2005) Industrial Restructuring and the State: The Case of MG Rover. *Local Economy*, 20, 360–371.

Blauberger, M. (2009) Compliance with Rules of Negative Integration: European State Aid Control in the New Member States. *Journal of European Public Policy*, 16, 1030–1046.

Boyer, R. (2000) The Unanticipated Fallout of the European Monetary Union: The Political and Institutional Deficits of the Euro. In Boyer, R. and Drache, D. (Eds.) *States Against Markets: The Limits of Globalization.* London, Routledge.

Brachinger, H. W. (2006) *Euro or "Teuro": The Euro-introduced Perceived Inflation in Germany.* Department of Quantitative Economics, University of Fribourg, Switzerland.

Bull, H. (1977) *The Anarchical Society.* New York, Columbia University Press.

Bulmer, S. (1986) *The Domestic Structure of European Community Policy-making in West Germany.* New York, Garland.

Burgess, M. (2000) *Federalism and the European Union: The Building of Europe, 1950–2000.* London, Routledge.

Burley, A.-M. and Mattli, W. (1993) Europe before the Court: A Political Theory of Legal Integration. *International Organization*, 47, 41–76.

Camerra-Rowe, P. (2004) Changing Patterns of Business Representation in the European Union. *Biennial Meeting of the Council for European Studies.* Chicago, IL.

Carr, E. H. (1964) *The Twenty Years' Crisis, 1919–1939.* New York, Harper & Row.

Carrubba, C. A. (2005) Courts and Compliance in International Regulatory Regimes. *Journal of Politics*, 67, 669–689.

Carrubba, C. A., Gabel, M. and HanklA, C. (2008) Judicial Behavior under Political Constraints: Evidence from the European Court of Justice. *American Political Science Review*, 102, 435–452.

Chayes, A. and Chayes, A. H. (1995) *The New Sovereignty: Compliance with International Regulatory Agreements.* Cambridge, MA, Harvard University Press.

Chayes, A., Chayes, A. H. and Mitchell, R. (1998) Managing Compliance: A Comparative Perspective. In Weiss, E. B. and Jacobson, H. K. (Eds.) *Engaging Countries: Strengthening Compliance with International Environmental Accords.* Cambridge, MA, MIT Press.

Checkel, J. T. (2001) The Europeanization of Citizenship? In Cowles, M. G., Caporaso, J. and Risse, T. (Eds.) *Transforming Europe: Europeanization and Domestic Change.* Ithaca, NY, Cornell University Press.

Cini, M. and Mcgowan, L. (2009) *Competition Policy in the European Union.* London, Palgrave Macmillan.

Cohen, B. (2003) Global Currency Rivalry: Can the Euro Ever Challenge the Dollar? *Journal of Common Market Studies*, 41, 575–595.

Collignon, S. and Mundschenk, S. (1999) The Sustainability of Public Debt in Europe. *Economica Internazionale*, 52, 101–159.

Conant, L. (2002) *Justice Contained.* Ithaca, NY, Cornell University Press.

Cowles, M. G., Caporaso, J. and Risse, T. (Eds.) (2001) *Transforming Europe: Europeanization and Domestic Change.* Ithaca, NY, Cornell University Press.

Crouch, C. and Streeck, W. (Eds.) (1997) *Political Economy of Modern Capitalism: Mapping Convergence in the Wake of European Monetary Union.* Oxford, Oxford University Press.

Dai, X. (2005) Why Comply? The Domestic Constituency Mechanism. *International Organization*, 59, 363–398.

Dai, X. (2007) *International Institutions and National Policies.* Cambridge, UK, Cambridge University Press.

Deeg, R. (1999) *Finance Capitalism Unveiled.* Ann Arbor, MI, University of Michigan Press.

Diamond, L. (1999) *Developing Democracy: Toward Consolidation.* Baltimore, MD, The Johns Hopkins University Press.

Döring, T. (2003) German Public Banks under the Pressure of the EU Subsidy Proceedings. *Intereconomics*, 38, 94–101.

Downs, G. W. (1998) Enforcement and the Evolution of Cooperation. *Michigan Journal of International Law*, 319–344.

Downs, G. W. and Rocke, D. M. (1995) *Optimal Imperfection? Domestic Uncertainty and Institutions in International Relations.* Princeton, NJ, Princeton University Press.

Downs, G. W. and Jones, M. A. (2002) Reputation, Compliance and International Law. *Journal of Legal Studies*, 31.

Downs, G. W. and Trento, A. W. (2004) Conceptual Issues Surrounding the Compliance Gap. In Luck, E. C. and DoylE, M. W. (Eds.) *International Law and Organization.* New York, Rowman & Littlefield.

Downs, G. W., Rocke, D. M. and Barsoom, P. N. (1996) Is the Good News about Compliance Good News about Cooperation? *International Organization*, 50, 379–406.

Duina, F. (1997) Explaining Legal Implementation in the European Union. *International Journal of the Sociology of Law*, 25, 155–179.

Duina, F. (1999) *Harmonizing Europe: Nation-states within the Common Market.* New York, State University of New York Press.

Dyson, K. (2000) *The Politics of the Euro—zone.* Oxford, Oxford University Press.

Dyson, K. (Ed.) (2002) *European States and the Euro.* Oxford, Oxford University Press.

Dyson, K. and Featherstone, K. (1999) *The Road to Maastricht.* Oxford, UK, Oxford University Press.

Ehrlich, S. D. (2007) Access to Protection: Domestic Institutions and Trade Policy. *International Organization*, 61, 571–605.

Eling, K. (1999) *The Politics of Cultural Policy in France.* London, St Martin's Press.

Esping-Andersen, G. (1990) *The Three Worlds of Welfare Capitalism.* Princeton, NJ, Princeton University Press.

Evans, P., Jacobson, H. K. and Putnam, R. D. (Eds.) (1993) *Double-edged Diplomacy: International Bargaining and Domestic Politics.* Berkeley, CA, University of California Press.

Featherstone, K. and Radaelli, C. M. (Eds.) (2003) *The Politics of Europeanization.* Oxford, UK, Oxford University Press.

Finnemore, M. and Sikkink, K. (1998) International Norm Dynamics and Political Change. *International Organization*, 52, 887–917.

Fox, G. H. and Roth, B. R. (2000) (Eds.) *Democratic Governance and International Law.* Cambridge, UK, Cambridge University Press.

Franck, T. M. (1990) *The Power of Legitimacy among Nations.* New York, Oxford University Press.

Franck, T. M. (1995) *Fairness in International Law and Institutions.* Oxford, Clarendon Press.

Garrett, G. (1992) International Cooperation and Institutional Choice. *International Organization*, 46, 533–558.

Garrett, G. (1995) The Politics of Legal Integration in the European Union. *International Organization*, 49, 17–81.

Garrett, G. and Tsebelis, G. (1996) An Institutional Critique of Intergovernmentalism. *International Organization*, 50, 269–299.

Gillingham, J. (2003) *European Integration 1950–2003: Superstate or New Market Economy?* Cambridge, UK, Cambridge University Press.

Goldsmith, J. L. and Posner, E. A. (2005) *The Limits of International Law.* Oxford, UK, Oxford University Press.

Gordon, P. H. and Meunier, S. (2001) Globalization and French Cultural Identity. *French Politics, Culture and Society*, 19, 22–41.

Gourevitch, P. (1986) *Politics in Hard Times.* Ithaca, Cornell University Press.

Grant, W. and Sargent, J. (1987) *Business and Politics in Britain.* London, Macmillan.

Greenwood, J. (1997) *Representing Interests in the European Union.* Basingstoke, Palgrave Macmillan.

Greenwood, J., Grote, J. and Ronit, K. (Eds.) (1992) *Organized Interests and the European Community.* New York, Routledge.

Grossman, E. (2006) Europeanization as an Interactive Process: German Public Banks meet EU State Aid Policy. *Journal of Common Market Studies*, 44, 325–348.

Gruber, L. (2000) *Ruling the World: Power Politics and the Rise of Supranational Institutions.* Princeton, NJ, Princeton University Press.

Guldager, P. (1997) Convergence of the EU Member States towards the EMU Requirements. *European Journal of Political Economy*, 13, 247–259.

Guzman, A. T. (2002) A Compliance-based Theory of International Law. *California Law Review*, 90, 1822–1887.

Guzman, A. T. (2008) *How International Law Works.* Oxford, UK, Oxford University Press.

Haas, E. (1958) *The Uniting of Europe.* Stanford, CA, Stanford University Press.

Haas, P. M. (1992) Introduction: Epistemic Communities and International Policy Coordination. *International Organization*, 46, 1–35.

Haas, P. M., Keohane, R. O. and Levy, M. A. (Eds.) (1993) *Institutions for the Earth: Sources of Effective International Environmental Protection.* Cambridge, MA, MIT Press.

Hall, P. A. (1986) *Governing the Economy.* Cambridge, Polity Press.

Hall, P. A. and Soskice, D. (Eds.) (2001) *Varieties of Capitalism.* Oxford, Oxford University Press.

Hallerberg, M. (2004) *Domestic Budgets in a United Europe.* Ithaca, NY, Cornell University Press.

Harvey, A. and Friedman, B. (2006) The Limits of Judicial Independence: The Supreme Court's Constitutional Rulings, 1987–2000. *Legislative Studies Quarterly*, 31, 533–562.

Hayward, S. (2000) France. In Kindem, G. (Ed.) *The International Movie Industry.* Carbondale, Southern Illinois University Press.

Henkin, L. (1979) *How Nations Behave: Law and Foreign Policy.* New York, Columbia University Press.

Hoffmann, S. (1956) The Role of International Organization: Limits and Possibilities. *International Organization*, 10, 357–372.

Holsti, O. (1996) *Public Opinion and American Foreign Policy*. Ann Arbor, University of Michigan Press.

Hooghe, L. and Marks, G. (2001) *Multi-level Governance and European Integration*. Lanham, MA, Rowman & Littlefield.

Iida, K. (1993) When and How do Domestic Constraints Matter: Two-level Games with Uncertainty. *Journal of Conflict Resolution*, 37, 403–426.

Keck, M. E. and Sikkink, K. (1998) *Activists beyond Borders: Advocacy Networks in International Politics*. Ithaca, NY, Cornell University Press.

Keohane, R. (1984) *After Hegemony: Cooperation and Discord in the World Political Economy*. Princeton, NJ, Princeton University Press.

Knopf, J. W. (1998) *Domestic Society and International Cooperation*. Cambridge, UK, Cambridge University Press.

Koen, V. and Van Den Noord, P. (2005) Fiscal Gimmickry in Europe: Once-off Measures and Creative Accounting. *OECD Economics Department Working Paper*.

Koh, H. H. (1996) Transnational Legal Process: The 1994 Roscoe Pound Lecture. *Nebraska Law Review*, 191, 181–208.

Koh, H. H. (1997) Why do Nations Obey International Law? *Yale Law Journal*, 106, 2599–2659.

Kohler-Koch, B. and Rittberger, B. (Eds.) (2007) *Debating the Democratic Legitimacy of the European Union*. Plymouth, UK, Rowman & Littlefield.

Koremenos, B., Lipson, C. and Snidal, D. (2003) *The Rational Design of Institutions*. Cambridge, UK, Cambridge University Press.

Kratochwil, F. (1989) *Rules, Norms, and Decisions on the Conditions of Practical and Legal Reasoning in International Relations and Domestic Affairs*. Cambridge, Cambridge University Press.

Kwon, G.-H. (1998) Pretests on the Theory of Collective Action: The Olson and Zechauser Model and its Elaboration. *Economics and Politics*, 10, 37–62.

Legro, J. W. (1997) Which Norms Matter? Revisiting the "Failure of Internationalism". *International Organization*, 51, 31–63.

Leibfried, S. and Pierson, P. (1995) Semisovereign Welfare States. In LeibFRIED, S. and Pierson, P. (Eds.) *European Social Policy*. Washington, DC, Brookings Institution.

Lieshout, R. H., Segers, M. L. L. and VAN DER Vleuten, A. M. (2004) De Gaulle, Moravcsik, and the Choice for Europe. *Journal of Cold War Studies*, 6, 89–139.

Lipson, C. (1991) Why are Some International Agreements Informal? *International Organization*, 45, 495–538.

Majone, G. (1996) *Regulating Europe*. London, Routledge.

Majone, G. (2005) *Dilemmas of European Integration*. Oxford, Oxford University Press.

Mccubbins, M. D. and Schwartz, T. (1984) Congressional Oversight Overlooked: Police Patrols versus Fire Alarms. *American Journal of Political Science*, 28, 165–179.

Mclaughlin, A. and Maloney, W. (1996) Privatization as Industrial Policy: State Withdrawal from the British Motor Industry. *Public Administration*, 74, 435–452.

Mcnamara, K. (1998) *The Currency of Ideas*. Ithaca, NY, Cornell University Press.

Maduro, M. P. (1998) *We, the Court: The European Court of Justice and the European Economic Constitution: A Critical Reading of Article 30 of the EC Treaty*. Evanston, IL and Oxford, Hart Publishing.

March, J. G. and OLSEN, J. P. (1998) The Institutional Dynamics of International Political Orders. In Katzenstein, P. J., Keohane, R. and Krasner, S. D. (Eds.) *Exploration and Contestation in the Study of World Politics.* Cambridge, MA, MIT Press.

Mazzucelli, C. (1999) *France and Germany at Maastricht: Politics and Negotiations to Create the European Union.* London, Routledge.

Mbaye, H. A. D. (2001) Explaining Implementation Infringements in the European Union 1972–1993. *European Union Politics*, 2, 259–281.

Merlingen, M., Mudde, C. and Sedelmeier, U. (2001) The Right and the Righteous? European Norms, Domestic Politics, and the Sanctions against Austria. *Journal of Common Market Studies*, 30, 59–77.

Milner, H. and Rosendorff, B. P. (1997) Domestic Politics and International Trade Negotiations: Elections and Divided Government Constraints on Trade Liberalization. *Journal of Conflict Resolution*, 41, 117–146.

Milward, A. (1992) *The European Rescue of the Nation State.* Berkeley, CA, University of California Press.

Mitchell, S. M. and Hensel, P. R. (2007) International Institutions and Compliance. *American Journal of Political Science*, 51, 383–411.

Mo, J. (1995) Domestic Institutions and International Bargaining: The Role of Agent Veto in Two-level Games. *American Political Science Review*, 89, 914–924.

Moravcsik, A. (1991) Negotiating the Single European Act: National Interests and Conventional Statecraft in the European Community. *International Organization*, 45, 19–56.

Moravcsik, A. (1993) Preferences and Power in the European Community. *Journal of Common Market Studies*, 31, 473–524.

Moravcsik, A. (1997) Taking Preferences Seriously: A Liberal Theory of International Politics. *International Organization*, 51, 513–553.

Moravcsik, A. (1998) *The Choice for Europe.* Ithaca, Cornell University Press.

Morganthau, H. (1951) *Politics among Nations.* New York, Alfred Knopf.

Ohlsson, L. F. (2007) Statistical Implications of the Stability and Growth Pact: Creative Accounting and the Role of Eurostat. *Working Papers in Economics: Göteborg University School of Business, Economics and Law.*

Olson, M. (1965) *The Logic of Collective Action.* Cambridge, MA, Harvard University Press.

Olson, M. and Zechauser, R. (1966) An Economic Theory of Alliances. *Review of Economics and Statistics*, 48, 266–279.

Oneal, J. R. (1990a) Testing the Theory of Collective Action: NATO Defense Burdens, 1950–1984. *Journal of Conflict Resolution*, 34, 426–448.

Oneal, J. R. (1990b) The Theory of Collective Action: NATO Defense Burdens, 1950–1984. *International Organization*, 44, 379–402.

Panke, D. (2007) The European Court of Justice as an Agent of Europeanization? Restoring Compliance with EU Law. *Journal of European Public Policy*, 14, 847–866.

Panke, D. (2010) Why (Big) States Cannot Do what they Want: International Legalization at Work. *International Politics*, 47, 186–209.

Pollack, M. (1997) Delegation, Agency and Agenda Setting in the European Community. *International Organization*, 51, 99–134.

Posner, E. A. (2009) *The Perils of Global Legalism.* Chicago, University of Chicago Press.

Putnam, R. D. (1988) Diplomacy and Domestic Politics. *International Organization*, 42, 427–460.

Rabkin, J. A. (2005) *Law Without Nations? Why Constitutional Government Requires Sovereign States.* Princeton, NJ, Princeton University Press.

Radaelli, C. (1997) *The Politics of Corporate Taxation in the European Union.* London, Routledge.

Raustilia, K. (1995) The Domestication of International Commitments. Working Paper. Laxenburg, IIASA.

Reus-Smit, C. (2003) Politics and International Legal Obligation. *European Journal of International Relations*, 9, 591–625.

Reus-Smit, C. (2004) The Politics of International Law. In REUS-SMIT, C. (Ed.) *The Politics of International Law.* Cambridge, Cambridge University Press.

Risse, T. (2001) A European Identity? Europeanization and the Evolution of Nation-State Identities. In Cowles, M. G., Caporaso, J. and Risse, T. (Eds.) *Transforming Europe.* Ithaca, NY, Cornell University Press.

Rollet, B. (2005) Cultural Exception(s) in French Cinema. In Godin, E. and Chafer, T. (Eds.) *The French Exception.* New York, Berghahn Books.

Rometsch, D. and Wessels, W. (Eds.) (1996) *The European Union and the Member States.* Manchester, UK, Manchester University Press.

Rosenberg, G. N. (1993) *The Hollow Hope: Can Courts Bring About Social Change?* Chicago, University of Chicago Press.

Sandholtz, W. (1993) Choosing Union: Monetary Politics and Maastricht. *International Organization*, 47, 1–39.

Sandler, T. and Forbes, J. F. (1980) Burden Sharing, Strategy, and the Design of NATO. *Economic Inquiry*, 18, 425–444.

Scharpf, F. (1999) *Governing in Europe: Effective and Democratic.* Oxford, Oxford University Press.

Schimmelfennig, F. (2004) *The EU, NATO and the Integration of Europe: Rules and Rhetoric.* Cambridge, Cambridge University Press.

Schmidt, V. A. (1996) *From State to Market? The Transformation of French Business and Government.* New York, Cambridge University Press.

Schmidt, V. A. (2002) *The Futures of European Capitalism.* Oxford, Oxford University Press.

Schmidt, V. A. (2006) *Democracy in Europe.* Oxford, UK, Oxford University Press.

Schmitter, P. C. and KARL, T. L. (1991) What Democracy Is ... and Is Not. *Journal of Democracy*, 2, 75–88.

Schütterle, P. (2003) Enlargement: Pre-accession State Aid After Accession. *European State Aid Law Quarterly*, 2, 39–38.

Sikkink, K. (1993) Human Rights, Principled Issue Networks, and Sovereignty in Latin America. *International Organization*, 47, 411–441.

Simmons, B. (2009) *Mobilizing for Human Rights.* Cambridge, UK, Cambridge University Press.

Simmons, B. A. (2000) Legalization of International Monetary Affairs. *International Organization*, 54, 573–602.

Slaughter, A.-M. (1995) International Law in a World of Liberal States. *European Journal of International Relations*, 6, 503–538.

Slaughter, A.-M. (2004) *A New World Order.* Princeton, NJ, Princeton University Press.

Smith, M. P. (1997) The Commission Made me Do it: The European Commission as a Strategic Asset in Domestic Politics. In Nugent, N. (Ed.) *At the Heart of the Union: Studies of the European Commission.* London, Macmillan.

Smith, M. P. (2001a) Europe and the German Model: Growing Tensions or Symbiosis? *Germany Politics*, 10, 119–140.

Smith, M. P. (2001b) In Pursuit of Selective Liberalization: Single Market Competition and its Limits. *Journal of European Public Policy*, 8, 519–540.

Snidal, D. (1991) Relative Gains and the Pattern of International Cooperation. *American Political Science Review*, 85, 701–726.

Spector, D. (2009) *Competition Policy in the EU.* Oxford, UK, Oxford University Press.

Staton, J. (2006) Constitutional Review and the Selective Promotion of Case Results. *American Journal of Political Science*, 56, 98–112.

Steunenberg, B. (2006) Turning Swift Policy-making into Deadlock and Delay. *European Union Politics*, 7, 293–319.

Stone Sweet, A. (2000) *Governing with Judges.* Oxford, Oxford University Press.

Stone Sweet, A. (2004) *The Judicial Construction of Europe.* Oxford, Oxford University Press.

Stone Sweet, A. and Brunnel, T. (1998) Constructing a Supranational Constitution. *American Political Science Review*, 92, 63–81.

Streeck, W. (1992) *Social Institutions and Economic Performance: Studies in the Industrial Relations in Advanced Capitalist Economies.* London, Sage.

Tallberg, J. (2002) Paths to Compliance: Enforcement, Management, and the European Union. *International Organization*, 56, 609–643.

Treib, O. (2003) EU Governance, Misfit, and the Partisan Logic of Domestic Adaptation. *European Union Studies Association.* Nashville, TN.

Tsebelis, G. (1995) Decision Making in Political Systems. *British Journal of Political Science*, 25, 289–325.

Tsebelis, G. (1999) Veto Players and Law Production in Parliamentary Democracies. *American Political Science Review*, 93, 591–605.

Tsebelis, G. (2002) *Veto Players.* Princeton, NJ, Princeton University Press.

Underdal, A. (1998) Explaining Compliance and Defection: Three Models. *European Journal of International Relations*, 4, 5–20.

Urwin, D. (2000) *The European Rescue of the Nation State.* London, Routledge.

Vanberg, G. (2005) *The Politics of Constitutional Review in Germany.* Cambridge, UK, Cambridge University Press.

Verdun, A. (1996) An "Asymmetrical" Economic and Monetary Union in the EU. *Journal of European Public Policy*, 5, 527–533.

Von Hagen, J. and Harden, I. (2004) What do Deficits Tell Us about Debts? *CEPR Discussion Papers No. 4579.*

Von Hagen, J., Hallet, A. H. and Strauch, R. (2000) Budgetary Consolidation in EMU. *Center for Economic and Policy Research.*

Von Stein, J. (2005) Do Treaties Constrain or Screen? Selection Bias and Treaty Compliance. *American Political Science Review*, 99, 611–622.

Walton, J. and Ragin, C. (1990) Global and National Sources of Political Protest: Third World Responses to the Debt Crisis. *American Sociological Review*, 55, 876–890.

Weiler, J. H. H. (1982) The Community System: The Dual Character of Supranationalism. *Yearbook of European Law*, 1.

Weiler, J. H. H. (1991) The Transformation of Europe. *Yale Law Journal*, 100, 2403–2483.

Weiler, J. H. H. (1994) A Quiet Revolution. *Comparative Political Studies*, 26, 510–534.

Weiler, J. H. H. (1999) *The Constitution of Europe: "Do the New Clothes Have an Emperor?" and Other Essays on European Integration.* New York, Cambridge University Press.

Wheatley, S. (2010) *The Democratic Legitimacy of International Law.* Oxford, UK, Hart Publishing.

Wolf, D. (2005) State Aid Control at Different Levels. In Zürn, M. and Joerges, C. (Eds.) *Law and Governance in Postnational Europe.* Cambridge, UK, Cambridge University Press.

Young, O. (1992) The Effectiveness of International Institutions. In Rosenau, J. N. and Czempiel, E.-O. (Eds.) *Governance without Government.* Cambridge, Cambridge University Press.

Zürn, M. (2004) Global Governance and Legitimacy Problems. *Government and Opposition*, 39, 260–287.

Zürn, M. (2005) Introduction: Law and Compliance at Different Levels. In Zürn, M. and Joerges, C. (Eds.) *Law and Governance in Postnational Europe.* Cambridge, UK, Cambridge University Press.

Zürn, M. and Joerges, C. (Eds.) (2005) *Law and Governance in Postnational Europe.* Cambridge, UK, Cambridge University Press.

Zürn, M. and Neyer, J. (2005) Conclusions – The Conditions of Compliance. In Zürn, M. and Joerges, C. (Eds.) *Law and Governance in Postnational Europe.* Cambridge, UK, Cambridge University Press.

Index